Praise for *SA*

An author writes:

*"**Sara** is the heartwarming novel of a girl who discovers the secrets of creating a happy life. And as Sara discovers how to create a better life for herself by starting right where she lives—the reader also learns the same lessons. Magically, both are transformed.*

"Reading this refreshing and inspiring book can awaken all readers to the inner power they already have for creating the kind of life they've always wished for.

*"**Sara** is a book you will want to give to your family and friends because it conveys powerful messages about life in a manner that is easy to understand and digest.*

*"The authors' inspired writing weaves an enchanting spell that can change lives just by reading it. And while this is not specifically a 'children's book,' **Sara** is a life-transforming story for the child in each of us.*

"Powerful. Magical. Empowering. Read it."

A tax accountant writes:

"Sara is wonderful. I'm on my third reading! So much to learn from it. Gives me a wonderful lift upward!"

A ten-year-old writes:

"I just read your book. . . . It's the best book I've ever read in my whole life. I just wanted to thank you for writing it 'cause it's made the biggest change in my whole entire life."

A grandmother says:

"What an overwhelming feeling of joy and appreciation I am feeling. My granddaughter now keeps reading parts to us and to her friends . . . so clear and delightful!"

"This wonderful little book is a gem, elegant in its clarity of message. Its teachings fly straight to the heart, connecting to the Sara in each of us! A gentle, charming story, it is sometimes funny, often poignant, and most of all, wonderfully joyful. It will surely become a primer for students of well-being."

— **Audrey Harbur Bershen,** psychotherapist

And Abraham says:

"This book will help you to remember that you're an eternal being . . . and it will help you to discover the everlasting bond that connects joyous loved ones to one another."

Sara receives the Award of Excellence

Body Mind Spirit Magazine, one of the widest known publishers of New Thought materials, has recently informed us that our beloved *Sara* has received their Award of Excellence as one of last year's outstanding books in print. And, as such, has been included as one of the 46 books recognized in their magazine's *Books to Live By* selection.

Esther and I were most pleased to learn that our dear friend Louise Hay's Hay House publication of another dear friend, Alan Cohen's book, *A Deep Breath of Life,* has also received the recognition.

"Dear Mr. & Mrs. Hicks: It is my pleasure to inform you that [this book] has received a 1997 *Body Mind Spirit* Award of Excellence as one of 1996's outstanding books in print. . .

"Chosen from hundreds of excellent books in print in the areas of spirituality, natural healing, relationships and creativity . . . each book makes a valuable contribution to our self-knowledge and self-transformation. . . .We commend the authors for these outstanding works. . . ."

Esther and I feel both appreciative of, and blessed by, the recognition of our *Sara.*

— Jerry Hicks

SARA, Book 1

Sara Learns the Secret about the *Law of Attraction*

Other Hay House Titles by Esther and Jerry Hicks
(The Teachings of Abraham)

Books, Calendar, and Card Decks

The Amazing Power of Deliberate Intent (also available in Spanish)
Ask and It Is Given (also available in Spanish)
Ask and It Is Given Cards
Ask and It Is Given Perpetual Calendar (available July 2007)
The Astonishing Power of Emotions (available September 2007)
The Law of Attraction
Manifest Your Desires (available June 2008)
Sara, Book 2: Solomon's Fine Featherless Friends
Sara, Book 3: A Talking Owl Is Worth a Thousand Words
The Teachings of Abraham Well-Being Cards

CD Programs

The Amazing Power of Deliberate Intent (Parts I and II: two 4-CD sets)
Ask and It Is Given (Parts I and II: two 4-CD sets)
The Astonishing Power of Emotions (Parts I and II: two 4-CD sets)
The Law of Attraction (4-CD set)

Please visit Hay House USA: **www.hayhouse.com®**
Hay House Australia: **www.hayhouse.com.au**
Hay House UK: **www.hayhouse.co.uk**
Hay House South Africa: **orders@psdprom.co.za**
Hay House India: **www.hayhouseindia.co.in**

SARA, Book 1

Sara Learns the Secret about the *Law of Attraction*

Esther and Jerry Hicks

Illustrated by Caroline S. Garrett

HAY HOUSE, INC.
Carlsbad, California
London • Sydney • Johannesburg
Vancouver • Hong Kong • New Delhi

Published and distributed in the United States by: Hay House, Inc.: www.hayhouse.com • ***Published and distributed in Australia by:*** Hay House Australia Pty. Ltd.: www.hayhouse.com.au • ***Published and distributed in the United Kingdom by:*** Hay House UK, Ltd.: www.hayhouse.co.uk • ***Published and distributed in the Republic of South Africa by:*** Hay House SA (Pty), Ltd.: orders@psdprom.co.za • ***Distributed in Canada by:*** Raincoast: www.raincoast.com • ***Published in India by:*** Hay House Publishers India: www.hayhouseindia.co.in

First published in 1995 by Abraham-Hicks Publications: ISBN: 0-9621219-4-0

Library of Congress Control No.: 2006924804

ISBN: 978-1-4019-1158-4

10 09 08 07 5 4 3 2
1st edition, April 2007
2nd edition, April 2007

Printed in the United States of America

This book is dedicated to all of you who, in your desire for enlightenment and Well-being, have asked the questions this book has answered . . . and to the four delightful children of our children who are examples of what the book teaches . . . who are not yet asking because they have not yet forgotten.

Foreword

Here is an inspiring as well as inspired book about a child's experiential journey into unlimited joyousness. Sara is a shy, withdrawn ten-year-old girl who is not very happy. She has an obnoxious brother who constantly teases her, cruel and unfeeling classmates, and an apathetic attitude toward her schoolwork. In short, she represents a lot of kids in our society today. When I first read this book, I was struck by the similarities between Sara and my own ten-year-old. Sara is really a composite of all children.

Sara wants to feel good and happy and loving, but as she looks around, she doesn't find much to feel that way about. This all changes when she meets Solomon, a wise old owl, who shows her how to see things differently through the eyes of unconditional love. He teaches Sara how to always be in an atmosphere of pure, positive energy. She sees for the first time who she really is and her unlimited potential. You, as the reader, will realize this is so much more than a children's story. This is a blueprint for attaining the joy and happiness that are your birthright.

My whole family read this book, and we haven't been the same since. My husband, perhaps, was the most moved by it. He actually said that it had such a tremendous impact on him that he looks at life with new eyes. It's like being nearsighted your whole life and then finally getting glasses. Everything becomes crystal clear.

I cannot say enough good things about this life-transforming book. You will share in Sara's ups and downs on the way to greater heights of fulfillment and know that there is a Sara in all of us. If there is only one book you ever buy, make sure it is this one (it's for all ages). You won't regret it!

— Denise Tarsitano, in
the Rising Star Series

Preface

"People would rather be entertained than informed." That was, I believe, an observation of eminent publisher William Randolph Hearst. If so, then to inform in an entertaining manner would seem to be the most effective mode of conveying information, even information of great personal value.

Sara Learns the Secret about the Law of Attraction both entertains and informs as it flows to you—as per your state of attraction—through the Universal thought translation process of Esther and her word processor. Streams of impeccable wisdom and unconditional love—gently taught by Sara's very entertaining feathered mentor—blend with the currents of Sara's enlightening experiences with her family, peers, neighbors, and teachers to lift you to a new awareness of your natural state of well-being, and of your knowing that all is really well.

Consider who you are and why you're here as you're considering studying this book, and then, at the completion of your first leisurely reading, take note of how far and how fast you have progressed toward all that is important to you.

As a result of the clearer perspectives that you will have gained from this brief, simple, thought-provoking novel, expect to experience a new level of joyous fulfillment.

— Jerry Hicks

PART I

Sara Learns the Secret about the *Law of Attraction*

Chapter 1

Sara frowned as she lay in her warm bed, disappointed to find herself awake. It was still dark outside, but she knew it was time to get up. *I hate these short winter days,* Sara thought. *I wish I could just stay here until the sun comes up.*

Sara knew she had been dreaming. It was something very pleasant, although she had no idea now what the dream had been about.

I don't want to wake up yet, Sara thought, as she tried to adjust from her pleasant dream into the not-so-pleasant cold winter morning. Sara snuggled down deep into her warm bed and listened to hear if her mother was up and moving about yet. She pulled the blankets up over her head, and closed her eyes and tried to recall a piece of the very pleasant dream she had awakened from. It had been so delicious that Sara wanted more.

Darn. I really need to use the bathroom. I'll just hold still and relax, and maybe I won't notice.

Sara shifted her position, trying to delay the inevitable. *It's not working. Okay. I'm up. Another day. Big deal.*

Sara tiptoed down the hall into the bathroom, carefully stepping over the spot in the floor that always creaked, and quietly closed the door. She decided to put off flushing the toilet so that she could enjoy the luxury of actually being awake and alone. *Just five more minutes of peace and quiet,* Sara thought.

"Sara? Are you up? Come here and help me!"

"Might as well flush the toilet," Sara muttered. "Okay, I'll be right there!" she called to her mother.

She could never figure out how her mother always seemed to know what everyone in the house was doing. *She must have bugging devices hidden in every room,* Sara bitterly decided. She knew that wasn't really true, but her negative mental rampage was well under way, and it seemed that there was no stopping it.

I'm going to stop drinking anything before I go to bed. Better yet, from noon on, I won't drink anything. Then, when I wake up, I can just lie in bed and think, all to myself—and no one will know I'm awake.

I wonder how old you are when you stop enjoying your own thoughts? I know that it happens, because no one else is ever quiet. They can't be listening to their own thoughts, 'cause they're always talking or watching television, and when they get in the car, the first thing they do is turn the radio on. Nobody seems to like to be alone. They always want to be with somebody else. They want to go to a meeting or to a movie or to a dance or to a ball game. I'd like to put a blanket of quiet over everything so I could, just for a little while, hear myself think. I wonder if it's possible to be awake and not be bombarded with other people's noise.

I'm going to organize a club. People against OPN. Member requirements include: You can like others, but you do not need to talk to them. You can like watching others, but do not need to explain to anybody else what you saw. You have to like to be alone sometimes to just think your own thoughts. It's okay to want to help others, but you must be willing to keep that to a minimum, because that's a trap that will ruin you for sure. If you're too helpful, it's all over. They'll consume you with their ideas, and you won't have any time for yourself. You must be willing to lay low and watch others without them being aware of you.

I wonder if anybody else would like to join my club. No, that would ruin it! My club is about not needing clubs! It's about my life being important enough, interesting enough, fun enough, that I don't need anybody else.

"Sara!"

Startled, Sara blinked as she came back into the awareness that she was standing in front of the bathroom sink, blankly staring into the mirror, with her toothbrush halfheartedly moving around in her mouth.

"Are you going to stay in there all day? Let's get moving. We have lots to do!"

~~~

~~~

Chapter 2

"Sara, did you have something you wanted to say?" Sara jumped, becoming aware again as Mr. Jorgensen said her name.

"Yes, sir. I mean, about what, sir?" Sara stammered while the other 27 students in her classroom snickered.

Sara had never understood why they took such delight in someone else's embarrassment, but they never failed to do just that, laughing raucously as if something actually funny had happened. *What is funny about someone else feeling bad?* Sara just couldn't sort out the answer to that, but now wasn't the time to ponder that anyway, for Mr. Jorgensen was still holding her in the unbelievable spotlight of discomfort while her classmates looked on with exaggerated glee.

"Can you answer the question, Sara?"

More laughing.

"Stand up, Sara, and give us your answer."

Why is he being so mean? Is this really so important?

Five or six eager hands shot up around the classroom, as show-off classmates took further delight in making Sara look bad.

"No, sir," Sara whispered, slipping down into her seat.

"What did you say, Sara?" the teacher barked.

"I said, no, sir, I do not know the answer to the question," Sara said, a bit louder. But Mr. Jorgensen wasn't finished with Sara—not yet.

"Do you know the question, Sara?"

Sara's face flushed red with embarrassment. She didn't have the slightest idea what the question was. She had been deep in her own thoughts, truly in her own world.

"Sara, may I offer a suggestion to you?"

Sara didn't look up, because she knew that giving her permission or not giving it wouldn't stop Mr. Jorgensen.

"I suggest, young lady, that you spend more time thinking about the important things that are discussed here in this classroom, and less time gazing out of the window, wasting your time on idle, needless thoughts. Try to put something in that empty head of yours." More laughter.

Will this class never end?

And then the bell, finally the bell.

Sara walked slowly home, watching her red boots sinking into the white snow. Grateful for the snowfall. Grateful for the quiet. Grateful for an opportunity to retreat into the privacy of her own mind as she began her two-mile walk home.

She noticed that the water beneath the Main Street bridge was nearly completely covered with ice, and she thought about sliding down the riverbank to see how thick the ice was, but decided to do that on another day. She was able to see the water flowing beneath the ice, and she smiled as she pondered how many different faces this river showed throughout the year. This bridge, crossing this river, was her favorite part of her walk home. There was always something interesting happening here.

Once across the bridge, Sara looked up for the first time since leaving the school yard, and she felt a little twinge of sadness wash over her as she realized that her quiet walk in solitude was only two blocks from ending. She slowed her pace to savor the peace she had rediscovered, and then turned and walked backwards for a bit, looking back at the bridge.

"Oh well," she sighed softly, as she entered the graveled driveway to her house. She paused on the steps to kick at a large sheet of ice, loosening it with her boot and kicking it off into a snow bank. Then she pulled off her wet boots and went into the house.

Quietly closing the door, and hanging her heavy wet coat on the hook, Sara made as little noise as possible.

She wasn't at all like the other members of her family who usually called out a loud, penetrating "I'm home!" upon entering. *I'd like to be a hermit,* she concluded, walking through the living room into the kitchen. *A quiet, happy hermit, thinking, talking or not talking, getting to choose everything about my day. Yes!*

CHAPTER 3

Her only awareness—as she lay sprawled in front of her school locker on the mud-streaked floor—was that her elbow was hurting, really hurting.

Falling down is always such a shock. It happens so fast. One moment you're upright, moving quickly forward with some very deliberate intention of being in your seat when the final bell rings, and the next minute you're lying flat on your back, immobilized, stunned, and hurting. And the worst thing in the whole world is to fall down at school, where everybody can see you.

Sara looked up into a sea of gleeful-looking faces that were grinning, snickering, or laughing right out loud. *They act like nothing like this has ever happened to them.*

Once they figured out that there was nothing as exciting as a broken bone or bleeding flesh, or a victim writhing in pain, the crowd dissolved, and her ghoulish schoolmates went on with their own lives, making their way back to their classrooms.

A blue-sweatered arm reached down, and a hand took hers, pulling her into a sitting position, and a girl's voice said, "Are you okay? Do you want to stand up?"

No, Sara thought, *I want to disappear,* but since that wasn't likely, and since the crowd had already pretty much dissolved, Sara smiled weakly, and Ellen helped her to her feet.

Sara had never spoken with Ellen before, but she had seen her in the hallways. Ellen was two grades ahead of Sara, and she had only been at her school for about a year.

Sara really didn't know much about Ellen, but then that wasn't unusual. Older kids never interacted with younger ones. There was some kind of unwritten code against that. But Ellen always smiled easily, and even though she didn't seem to have many friends and moved about pretty much by herself, she seemed perfectly happy. That may have been why Sara had noticed her. Sara was a loner, too. She preferred it that way.

"These floors get so slippery when it's wet outside," Ellen said. "I'm surprised more people don't fall down in here."

Still a bit dazed, and embarrassed into numbness, Sara wasn't consciously focused on the words Ellen was speaking, but something about Ellen's offering was making Sara feel much better.

It was a little unsettling to Sara to find herself so affected by another person. It was truly a rare occasion for her to prefer the words spoken from another to the quiet retreat into her own private thoughts. This felt weird.

"Thank you," Sara murmured, as she tried to brush some of the mud from her soiled skirt.

"I don't think it will look so bad once it dries a bit," Ellen said.

And, again, it wasn't the words that Ellen spoke. They were just normal, everyday words, but it was something else. Something about the way she spoke them.

Ellen's calm, clear voice seemed to soothe the sense of tragedy and trauma Sara had been feeling, and her enormous embarrassment all but vanished, leaving Sara feeling stronger and better.

"Oh, it doesn't really matter." Sara replied. "We'd better hurry or we'll be late."

And as she took her seat—elbow throbbing, clothes muddied, shoelaces untied, and her stringy brown hair hanging in her eyes—she felt better than she had ever felt sitting in this seat. It wasn't logical, but it was true.

Sara's walk home from school was different that day. Instead of withdrawing into her own quiet thoughts, noticing not much more than the narrow path in the snow before her, Sara felt alert and alive. She felt like singing. So she did. Humming a familiar tune, she moved happily down her path, watching others on their way about the small town.

As she passed the town's only restaurant, Sara considered stopping in for an after-school snack. Often, a glazed doughnut or an ice-cream cone, or a small basket of French-fried potatoes, was just the thing to temporarily distract Sara from the long, weary day she had spent in school.

I still have all of this week's allowance, Sara thought, standing on the sidewalk in front of the small café, considering. But she decided not to, as she remembered her mother's often-offered words: "Don't spoil your dinner."

Sara had never understood those words because she was always ready to eat if what was offered was good. It was only when dinner didn't look good, or, more important, when it didn't smell good, that she found excuses to pass it by, or at least eat it sparingly. *Seems to me like somebody else is the one that spoils it.* Sara grinned to herself as she continued walking home. She really didn't need anything today, anyway—for today, all was really rather well in Sara's world.

~~~
~~~

Chapter 4

Sara stopped atop the Main Street bridge, looking below at the ice to see if it looked thick enough to walk across. She spotted a few birds standing on the ice and noticed some rather large dog tracks in the snow on the ice, but she didn't think that the ice was quite yet ready for all of her weight, including her heavy coat, boots, and a rather hefty bag of books. *Better wait a bit,* Sara thought, as she peered down the icy river.

Leaning way out over the ice, supported by the rusty railing, which Sara believed was there just for her own personal pleasure, and feeling better than she had felt in a long time, she decided to stay for a while to look at her wonderful river. She dropped her book bag to her feet and leaned against her rusty metal railing, Sara's favorite place in the whole world.

Resting and leaning and appreciating this spot, Sara smiled as she remembered the day this old railing was transformed into the perfect leaning perch by Mr. Jackson's hay truck when he slammed on his brakes on the wet, icy road to avoid running over Harvey, Mrs. Peterson's dachshund. Everyone in town talked on and on for months about how lucky he was that his truck didn't go right into the river. Sara was always surprised at how people were always making things seem bigger and worse than they really were. If Mr. Jackson's truck had gone into the river, well, that would be quite different. That would justify the big fuss everyone made. Or if he had gone into the river and had drowned, that would have been even more reason to talk. But he didn't go into the river.

As far as Sara could figure out, no harm had come from it at all. His truck wasn't damaged. Mr. Jackson wasn't damaged. Harvey was frightened and stayed home for several days, but he wasn't hurt in any way. *People just like to worry,* Sara concluded. But Sara was elated when she discovered her new leaning perch. Large, heavy-gauge steel posts were now bending way out over the water. So perfect, it was as if it was made especially to please and delight Sara.

Leaning out over the river and looking downstream, Sara could see the great log stretched across the river, and that made her smile, too. That was another "accident" that suited her just fine.

One of the big trees that lined the riverbank was badly damaged in a wind storm. So the farmer who owned the land gathered some volunteers from around town, and they trimmed all of the branches from the tree, getting ready to cut it down. Sara wasn't sure why there was so much excitement about it. It was just one big old tree.

Her father wouldn't let her get close enough to hear much of what they were saying, but Sara heard someone say that they were worried that the power lines might be too close. But then the big saws started buzzing again, and Sara couldn't hear anything else, so she stood back at a distance, with most everyone else in town, to watch the big event.

Suddenly, the saws were quiet and Sara heard someone shout, "Oh no!" Sara remembered covering her ears and squeezing her eyes closed tight. It felt like the whole town shook when the huge tree fell, but when Sara opened her eyes, she squealed with delight as she got her first glimpse of her perfect log bridge connecting the little dirt paths on each side of the river.

As Sara basked in her metal nest, hanging right out over the river, she breathed deeply, wanting to take in that great river smell. It was hypnotic. The fragrances, the constant, steady sound of the water. *I love this old river,* Sara thought, still gazing at her big log that was crossing the water downstream.

Sara loved to put her hands out for balance and see how quickly she could scoot across the log. She was never frightened, but she was always mindful that the slightest slip could take her tumbling into the river. And Sara never crossed the log that she didn't hear her mother's cautious, uncomfortable words playing in her mind: "Sara, stay away from that river! You could drown!"

But Sara didn't pay much attention to those words, not anymore, anyway, because she knew something that her mother didn't. Sara knew that she couldn't drown.

Relaxed, and at one with the world, Sara lay in her perch and remembered what had happened on that very log just two summers earlier. It had been late in the afternoon, and all of Sara's chores were done, so she had gone down to the river. She had leaned in her metal perch for a while, and then she had followed the dirt path down to the log. The river, swollen from the run-off from the melting snow, was higher than usual, and water was actually lapping up over the log. She had debated whether it was a good idea to cross over. But then, with a strange sort of whimsical enthusiasm, she decided to cross her precarious log bridge. As she got near the middle, she paused for a moment and turned sideways on the log with both feet pointing downstream, teetering back and forth only slightly, as she regained her balance and her courage. And then, from out of nowhere, came the Pittsfields' mangy mutt Fuzzy, bounding across the bridge, happily acknowledging Sara, and bumping up against her with sufficient force to topple Sara into the very fast-moving river.

Well, this is it, Sara had thought. *Just as my mother warned, I'm going to drown!* But things were moving too fast for Sara to give too much thought to that. For Sara found herself on an amazing and wonderful ride as she floated rapidly downstream on her back with eyes looking upward, seeing one of the most beautiful views she had ever witnessed.

She had walked these riverbanks hundreds of times, but this was a point of view very different from what she'd noticed before. Gently carried on this amazing cushion of water, she could see blue sky up above, framed by perfectly shaped trees, denser and sparser, thicker and thinner. So many beautiful shades of green.

Sara wasn't aware that the water was extremely cold, but instead, she felt as if she were floating on a magic carpet, smoothly and quietly and safely.

For a moment, it seemed to be getting darker. As Sara floated into a thick grove of trees that lined the riverbank, she could see almost no sky at all.

"Wow, these trees are beautiful!" Sara said right out loud. She had never walked this far downstream. The trees were lush and lovely, and some of their limbs were dipping right down into the river.

And then, a long, friendly, solid limb seemed to reach right down into the water to give Sara a hand up.

"Thank you, tree," Sara said sweetly, pulling herself out of the river. "That was very nice of you."

She stood on the riverbank, dazed but exhilarated, and tried to get her bearings.

Wow! Sara murmured as she spotted the Petersons' big red barn. She could barely believe her eyes. In what had seemed to Sara like only a minute or two, she had floated over five miles through pastures and farmland. But Sara didn't mind the long walk home one bit. With delicious enthusiasm for life, Sara walked and skipped her way home.

As soon as she could get out of them, she put her dirty, wet clothes in the washing machine and hurriedly ran a nice warm bath. *No point in giving Mother one more thing to worry about,* she had thought. *This won't make her feel safer.*

Sara lay back in the warm water, smiling, as all sorts of leaves and dirt and river bugs washed out of her curly brown hair, knowing, with certainty, that her mother was wrong.

Sara knew that she would never drown.

∾∾∾

CHAPTER 5

"Sara, wait up!" Sara stopped in the center of the intersection and waited as her little brother ran at top speed toward her.

"Ya gotta come, Sara, it's real neat!"

I'll bet it is, Sara thought, pondering the last several "real neat" things Jason had sprung on her. There was the barn rat he'd trapped in his own self-made trap, that "really was alive last time I looked," Jason had promised. Twice, he'd caught Sara off guard and had tricked her into peering into his school bag, only to find some innocent little bird or mouse that had fallen prey to Jason and his grungy little friends, excited and eager to use their new Christmas BB guns.

What is it with boys? Sara pondered, waiting, as Jason, tired, had now slowed to a walk, seeing that Sara was actually waiting for him. *How can they actually take pleasure in hurting poor, defenseless little animals? I'd like to catch them in a trap and see how they like it,* Sara thought. *I remember when his pranks were less gory and even funny, sometimes, but Jason just seems to get meaner and meaner.*

Sara stood in the middle of the quiet country road waiting for her brother to catch up to her. She suppressed a smile as she remembered the clever hoax Jason had carried out by laying his head down on his desk, hiding his shiny rubber vomit, and then looking up with his big brown eyes, exposing his sickening prize when his teacher stood over him. Mrs. Johnson had rushed out of the room to get the janitor to deal with the mess, but when she came back, Jason announced that he had taken care of it, and Mrs. Johnson was so relieved that she didn't even ask any questions. Jason was excused to go home.

Sara was stunned at how gullible Mrs. Johnson had been, not even wondering how this vomit, which appeared fresh and runny, managed to stand in such a neat little puddle on a desk with a fairly significant slope. But then, Mrs. Johnson hadn't yet had as much experience with Jason as Sara had, and, she admitted, he got to her more than once, in her more naive days, but no more. Sara was on to her brother.

"Sara!" Jason shouted, winded and excited.

Sara stepped back, "Jason, you don't have to yell, I'm only two feet away from you."

"Sorry." Jason gulped as he tried to catch his breath. "You gotta come! Solomon's back!"

"Who's Solomon?" Sara questioned, regretting her question as soon as it was blurted out; she didn't want to show one bit of interest in whatever Jason was babbling about.

"Solomon! You know, *Solomon.* The giant bird on Thacker's Trail!"

"I never heard of a giant bird on Thacker's Trail," Sara offered, mustering as much of a sound of boredom as she could on such short notice. "Jason, I'm not interested in any more of your stupid birds."

"This bird isn't stupid, Sara, it's gigantic! You should see it. Billy said it's bigger than his father's car. Sara, you have to come, please."

"Jason, a bird cannot be bigger than a car."

"Yes, it can! You can ask Billy's dad! He was driving home one day, and he said he saw a shadow so big he thought it was an airplane passing over him. It covered the whole car. But it wasn't an airplane, Sara, it was Solomon!"

Sara had to admit that Jason's enthusiasm for Solomon was getting to her a bit.

"I'll go some other time, Jason. I have to get home."

"Oh, Sara, please come! Solomon might not be here again. You have to come, Sara, you have to!"

Jason's persistence was beginning to worry Sara. He wasn't usually so intense. Ordinarily, when he felt Sara's strong will kicking in, he'd just give up and lay low and wait for another opportunity to catch her more off guard. He'd learned, from much experience, that the more he pressed his sister to do something that she didn't want to do, the more impossible Sara became. But there was something different here. Jason seemed compelled in a way that Sara hadn't seen before, and so, to Jason's tremendous surprise and delight, Sara gave in.

"Oh, all right, Jason. Where is this giant bird?"

"His name is Solomon."

"How do you know his name?"

"Billy's dad named him. He says he's an owl. And owls are wise. So his name should be Solomon."

Sara picked up her pace to try to keep up with Jason. *He's really excited about this bird,* Sara thought. *This is weird.*

"He's in here, somewhere," Jason said. "He lives in here."

Sara was often amused at Jason's assumed confidence, when Sara knew that he knew that he really didn't know what he was talking about. But, more often than not, Sara would play along, pretending that she didn't notice. It was easier that way.

They looked into the sparsely leafed thicket, now covered with snow. They walked along a badly decaying fence row, following a narrow path in the snow, carved out by a lone dog that had apparently run along not long before them. . . .

Sara almost never walked this path in the winter. It was out of the way of her usual walk between school and home. This was, however, a place where Sara had spent countless blissful summer hours. Sara walked along, noting all the familiar nooks and crannies, feeling good about revisiting her old path. *Best thing about this path,* Sara thought, *is that I had it mostly to myself. No cars passing, no neighbors. This is a quiet path. I should walk here more often.*

"Solomon!" Jason's voice rang out, startling Sara. She hadn't expected him to shout.

"Jason, don't yell at Solomon. If he is in here, he won't be if you keep that up."

"He is in here, Sara. I told you, he lives in here. And if he woulda left, we woulda seen him. He's really big, Sara, really!"

Sara and Jason walked deeper and deeper into the thicket, ducking under a rusty wire, which was one of the last remnants of this rickety old fence. They walked along slowly, feeling their way carefully, not certain what might be buried in this knee-deep snow.

"Jason, I'm getting cold."

"Just a little more, Sara. Please?"

It was more from her own curiosity than from Jason's prodding, but Sara agreed. "Okay, Jason, five more minutes!" Sara shrieked as she stepped, waist-high, into an irrigation ditch camouflaged by the snow. The cold, wet snow came right up under Sara's coat and blouse and touched right up against her bare skin. "Okay, Jason, that's it! I'm going home!"

Jason was disappointed that they didn't find Solomon, but Sara's irritation had distracted him from that. There wasn't much that pleased Jason more than his sister's irritation. Jason laughed heartily as Sara shook the cold wet snow out from under her clothing.

"Oh, you think that's funny, don't you, Jason? You probably made this whole Solomon thing up just to get me wet and mad!"

Jason laughed as he ran out ahead of Sara. As much as he enjoyed her irritation, he had wisely learned to keep a safe distance. "No, Sara, Solomon is real. You'll see."

"Yeah, right!" Sara snapped back at Jason.

But for some reason, Sara knew that Jason was right.

~~~

~~~

Chapter 6

Sara couldn't remember a time that it was easy for her to concentrate on what was going on in the classroom. *School is truly the most boring place on earth,* she had concluded long ago. But this day, without exception, was the hardest that Sara had ever experienced. She couldn't keep her mind on what the teacher was saying. Her mind kept drifting back to the thicket. And as soon as the last bell rang, Sara stuffed her book bag into her locker and went directly there.

"I'm probably crazy," Sara murmured to herself, as she walked deeper and deeper into the thicket, making her own trail in the deep snow as she moved along. "I'm looking for a silly bird that's probably not even real. Well, if I don't see him right away, I'm leaving. I don't want Jason to know that I'm here, or that I'm even interested in this bird."

Sara stopped to listen. It was so still that she could hear her own breathing. She couldn't see one other living creature. Not a bird, not a squirrel. Nothing. In fact, if it were not for the tracks that Sara and Jason and the lone dog had left there yesterday, Sara might have thought she was, indeed, the only one alive on the planet.

This was truly a beautiful winter day. The sun had been shining brightly all afternoon, and the top crust of the snow was shiny and wet as it was slowly melting. Everything was glistening. Ordinarily, a day like this would make Sara's heart sing. What could be better than to be off, all alone, thinking her own thoughts on a beautiful day like this? But Sara felt irritated. She had hoped that Solomon would be easy to find. Somehow, thinking about the thicket and the possibility of spotting this mysterious bird had piqued Sara's interest, but now, standing here alone, knee-deep in snow, Sara began to feel foolish. "Where is this bird? Oh, forget it! I'm going home!"

In her frustration, Sara stood in the middle of the thicket, feeling angry and overwhelmed and somewhat confused. She started backtracking out of the thicket, the way she had come in, but then stopped to consider if it would be faster to cross through the pasture that she so often used as a shortcut during the summer months. *I'm sure the river is frozen over by now. Maybe I can cross it here somewhere where it's narrow,* Sara thought, as she ducked under the single wire fence.

Sara was surprised by how disoriented she was here in the winter. She had passed through this pasture hundreds of times. This was the pasture where her uncle kept his horse during the summer months, but everything looked very different with all of her familiar landmarks buried beneath the snow. The river was completely iced over here, and was covered by several inches of snow. Sara stopped, trying to remember where the narrowest point was. And then she felt the ice giving way beneath her feet—and before she knew it, she was flat on her back on the very tentative ice with cold water quickly soaking through her clothes. Sara flashed back to the amazing ride this river had given her before, and, for a moment, she felt real panic, imagining a repeat of that ride, but in this freezing cold water, being carried downstream to a frozen death.

Have you forgotten that you cannot drown? A kind voice spoke from somewhere over Sara's head.

"Who's there?" Sara asked, looking all around, staring up into the bare trees, squinting from the glare of the sun that was glistening and reflecting off of the snow-covered everything around her. *Whoever you are, why don't you help me out of here?* Sara thought, as she lay on the cracking ice, frightened that any movement might cause the ice to give way beneath her.

The ice will hold you. Just roll over onto your knees and crawl over here, her mysterious friend said.

So, without looking up, Sara rolled over onto her stomach, and ever so slowly she pulled herself up onto her knees.

And then, gingerly, she began crawling in the direction of the voice.

Sara was in no mood for conversation. Not now. She was wet and very cold, and really mad at herself for doing something so stupid. What she was most interested in, right now, was getting home and changing before anyone else came home and caught her in her telltale clothes.

"I've gotta go," Sara said, squinting into the sun in the direction of whomever she had been talking to.

She began picking her way back through her own tracks, very cold, and irritated by her decision to try to cross the silly river. And then it hit her. "Hey, how'd *you* know that I can never drown?" No answer came back to her.

"Where'd you go? Hey, where are you?" Sara called.

And then the biggest bird Sara had ever seen took flight from the treetop, soared high into the sky, circled the thicket and pastures below, and disappeared into the sun.

Sara stood in amazement, squinting into the sunlight. *Solomon.*

~~~

~~~

Chapter 7

Sara awakened the next morning, and as usual, ducked back under the covers, bracing against beginning another day. Then she remembered Solomon.

Solomon, Sara thought, *did I really see you, or did I dream you?*

But then, as Sara woke up more, she remembered going to the thicket after school to look for Solomon, and the ice giving way beneath her feet. *No, Solomon, you were not a dream. Jason was right. You're real.*

Sara flinched as she thought of Jason and Billy shouting their way through the thicket looking for Solomon. And then that heavy, flustered feeling that Sara always got when she thought of Jason blasting into her life swept over her.

I won't tell Jason or anyone that I've seen Solomon. This is my secret.

Sara struggled all day long to give her attention to her teacher. Her mind kept pulling back to the glistening thicket and this gigantic, magical bird. *Did Solomon actually speak to me?* Sara pondered. *Or did I only imagine it? Maybe I was dazed from falling. Maybe I was unconscious and dreamed it. Or did it happen?*

Sara could hardly wait to go to the thicket again to find out if Solomon was real.

When the last bell rang, Sara stopped by her locker to deposit her books and then stuffed her book bag on top of them. This may have been the second day ever that Sara didn't lug home all of her books. She had discovered that an armload of books seemed to protect her from any intrusive classmates. They somehow provided a barrier that kept frivolous, playful intruders out of her way. But today, Sara didn't want anything to slow her down. She shot out of the front doors like a bullet, heading straight for Thacker's Trail.

As Sara left the paved street and started down the trail, she saw a very large owl sitting in plain view on a fence post right out in the open. It almost seemed as if he were waiting for her. Sara was surprised to find Solomon so easily. She had spent so much time searching for this illusive mystery bird, and now here he was, just sitting there as if he'd always been right there.

Sara didn't know quite how to approach Solomon. *What should I do?* Sara thought. *It seems odd to just walk up to a big owl and say,* 'Hello, how are you today?'

Hello, how are you today? the big owl said to Sara.

Sara jumped back about a foot. Solomon laughed heartily. *I didn't mean to startle you, Sara. How are you today?*

"I'm fine, thank you. I'm just not used to talking to owls, that's all."

Oh, that's too bad, Solomon said. *Some of my very best friends are owls.*

Sara laughed. "Solomon, you're funny."

Solomon, hmmmm, the owl said. *Solomon is a nice name. Yes, I think I like it.*

Sara blushed with embarrassment. She had forgotten that they had never really been introduced. Jason had told Sara the owl was named Solomon. But Billy's father had chosen that name. "Oh, I'm very sorry," Sara said. "I should have asked you your name."

Well, I've never actually thought about that, the owl said. *Solomon is a nice name however. I do like that.*

"What do you mean, you've never thought about it? Don't you have a name?"

No, not really, the owl replied.

Sara couldn't believe her ears. "How can you not have a name?"

Well, you see, Sara, only people need labels to identify things. The rest of us just seem to know who we are, and the labels are not that important to us. But I do like the name Solomon. And since you're accustomed to calling others by name, that one will do nicely for me. Yes, I do like that name. Solomon, it is.

Solomon seemed so pleased with his new name that Sara's embarrassment went away. Name or no name, this bird was certainly pleasant to talk with.

"Solomon, do you think I should tell anybody about you?"

Perhaps. In time.

"But you think I should keep you a secret for now, right?"

That's best for a while. Until you figure out what you would say.

"Oh, yeah, I guess I would sound pretty silly. 'I've got this owl friend who talks to me without moving his lips.'"

And I might **wisely** *point out to you, Sara, that owls do not have lips.*

Sara laughed. This was a very funny bird. "Oh, Solomon, you know what I mean. How do you talk without using your mouth? And how come I've never heard anybody else around here talking about you?"

No one else around here has ever heard me. It's not the sound of my voice you're hearing, Sara. ***You're receiving my thoughts.***

"I don't understand. I can hear you!"

Well, it seems like you're hearing me, and, truly, you are, but not with your ears. Not in the way you hear some other things.

Sara pulled her scarf up around her neck and pulled her stocking cap down over her ears, as a blast of cold wind swept around her.

It will be dark soon, Sara. We can visit more tomorrow. Think about what we talked about. While you are dreaming tonight, notice that you can see. Even though your eyes will be closed tight, you will see in your dreams. ***So, if you do not need your eyes to see, you also do not need your ears to hear.***

Before Sara could point out that dreams are different from real life, Solomon said, *Good-bye, Sara. Isn't this a lovely day?* And with that, Solomon leaped into the air, and pulling with his powerful wings, he rose high above the thicket and his fence post and his tiny friend below.

Solomon, Sara thought, *you're gigantic!*

Sara remembered Jason's words: "He's gigantic, Sara, you have to come and see him!" As she made her way home through the snow, she remembered how he nearly dragged Sara to the thicket, literally running with excitement, making it hard for Sara to keep up with him.

Strange, Sara pondered, *he was so intense about me seeing this gigantic bird, and now, in three days, he has not said one word about it. I'm surprised that he and Billy have not been out here every single day looking for Solomon. It's as though he has forgotten all about it. I'll have to remember to ask Solomon about that tomorrow.*

Over the next few days, Sara often found herself saying, "I'll have to ask Solomon about that." In fact, she had started to carry a little notebook in her pocket so she could make notes about the subjects she wanted to discuss.

It seemed that there was never enough time to talk to Solomon about all the things she wanted to ask him about. The narrow window of time between school ending and Sara needing to be home to complete her after-school chores before her mother came home from work was little more than 30 minutes.

—ʊʊ—

It's not fair, Sara had begun to think. *I spend all day with boring teachers who aren't one-tenth as smart as Solomon, and a measly half hour with the smartest teacher I've ever had. Hmm, teacher. I have an owl for a teacher.* That made Sara laugh right out loud.

"I'll have to ask Solomon about that."

~~~
~~~

Chapter 8

"Solomon, are you a teacher?"

Yes, indeed, Sara.

"But you don't talk about things that 'real' teachers, excuse me, 'other' teachers talk about. I mean, you talk about things that I'm interested in. You talk about neat stuff."

Actually, Sara, I talk only about that which you talk about. Only when you ask a question is the information that I might offer of any value to you. All of those answers that are offered without a question having been asked are truly a waste of everyone's time. Neither student nor teacher has much fun in that.

Sara thought about what Solomon had said, and she realized that unless Sara asked about it, Solomon didn't talk much about anything. "But wait, Solomon. I remember something you said without my asking a question."

And what was that, Sara?

"You said, 'Have you forgotten that you cannot drown?' It was the very first thing you said to me, Solomon. I didn't say a word to you. I was lying there on the ice, but I wasn't asking you a question."

Ah, it seems that Solomon is not the only one around here who can talk without moving his lips.

"What do you mean?"

You were asking, Sara, but not with words. Questions are not always asked with words.

"That's weird, Solomon. How can you ask something if you're not talking?"

By thinking your question. Many beings and creatures communicate through thought. In fact, more communicate that way than with words. People are the only ones who use words. But even they do much more of their communicating with thoughts than with words. Think about it.

You see, Sara, I am a wiiiiiiiiise old teacher whoooooo learned long ago that giving a student information that he or she is not asking for is a waste of time.

Sara laughed at Solomon's corny emphasis on *wise* and his owl-like exaggerated *whoooooo. I love this crazy bird,* Sara thought.

I love you too, Sara, Solomon replied.

Sara blushed, having forgotten already that Solomon could hear her thoughts.

And then, with no further words, Solomon lifted powerfully into the sky and was gone from Sara's view.

~~~

~~~

Chapter 9

"I wish I could fly like you, Solomon."

Why, Sara? Why would you like to fly?

"Oh, Solomon, it's so boring to have to walk around down here on the ground all the time. It's so slow. It just takes forever to get places, and you can't see much either. Only stuff that's down here on the ground with you. Boring stuff."

Well, Sara, it seems like you haven't really answered my question.

"Yes, I did, Solomon. I said I want to fly because . . ."

Because you don't like to walk around down here on the boring ground. You see, Sara, you didn't tell me why you want to fly. You told me why you don't want not *to fly.*

"There's a difference?"

Oh yes, Sara. A big difference. Try again.

A little surprised at Solomon's new decision to nitpick, Sara began again. "Okay. I want to fly because walking isn't much fun, and it takes so long to walk around down here on the ground."

Sara, can you see that you're still talking more about what you don't want and why you don't want it? Try again.

"Okay. I want to fly because . . . I don't get this, Solomon. What do you want me to say?"

I want you to talk about what you ***do*** *want, Sara.*

"I want to fly!" Sara shouted, feeling annoyed at Solomon's inability to understand her.

Now, Sara, tell me why you want to fly. What would that be like? How would it feel? Make it feel real to me, Sara. Describe to me, what does flying feel like? I don't want you to tell me what it's like down on the ground, or what it is like ***not*** *to fly. I want you to tell me what it's like to fly.*

Sara closed her eyes, now catching the spirit of what Solomon was getting at, and began to speak. "Flying feels very free, Solomon. It's like floating, but faster."

Tell me, what would you see if you were flying?

"I would see the whole town down below. I would see Main Street and cars moving and people walking. I would see the river. I would see my school."

How does flying feel, Sara? Describe what it feels like to fly.

Sara paused with her eyes closed and pretended that she was flying high above her town. "It would be so much fun, Solomon! Flying just has to be so much fun. I could soar as fast as the wind. It would feel so free. It feels so good,

Solomon!" Sara continued, now completely absorbed in her imagined vision. And then, suddenly, with the same sense of power that Sara had felt in Solomon's wings as she had seen him lift off his post day after day, Sara felt a whoosh within her that took her breath away. Her body felt, for a moment, as if it weighed 10,000 pounds, and then, instantly, she felt absolutely weightless. Sara was flying.

"Solomon," Sara squealed with delight, "look at me, I'm flying!"

Solomon was flying right along with her, and together they soared high above Sara's town, the town where Sara was born, the town that Sara had walked nearly every square inch of, the town that Sara was now discovering from a vantage point she had never dreamed possible.

"Wow! Solomon, this is great! Oh, Solomon, I love this!"

Solomon smiled and enjoyed Sara's extraordinary enthusiasm.

"Where are we going, Solomon?"

You may go wherever you'd like to go.

"Oh, wow!" Sara blurted, looking down at her quiet little town. It had never looked so beautiful before.

Sara had seen her town from the air once when her uncle had taken Sara and her family up in his small airplane, but she hadn't really been able to see much. The windows in the airplane were so high, and every time she got up on her knees to get her face closer to the window for a better view, her father had told her to sit back down and buckle her seat belt. She really didn't have much fun that day.

But this was very different. She could see everything. She could see every street and building in her town. She could see the few tiny businesses sprawled out along Main Street . . . Hoyt's Grocery Store and Pete's Drug Store and the Post Office. . . . She could see her beautiful river winding its way through the town. And a few cars were moving about, and a handful of people were walking here and there.

"Oh, Solomon," Sara said breathlessly, "this is the absolute best thing that has ever happened to me. Let's go to my school, Solomon. I'll show you where I spend my da . . ." Sara's voice trailed off as she sped off toward her school.

"The school looks so different from up here!" Sara was surprised at how large her school looked. The roof seemed like it went on forever. "Wow!" Sara exclaimed. "Can we go down closer, or do we have to stay way up here?"

You may go wherever you want to go, Sara.

Sara squealed once again and swooped down over the playground and slowly past her classroom window. "This is great! Look, Solomon! You can see my desk, and there's Mr. Jorgensen."

Sara and Solomon soared from one end of Sara's town to the other, swooping down close to the ground and then soaring back up, almost touching the clouds. "Look, Solomon, there's Jason and Billy."

"Hey, Jason, look at me, I'm flying!" Sara shouted. But Jason didn't hear. "Hey, Jason!" Sara shouted again, more loudly. "Look at me! I'm flying!"

Jason cannot hear you, Sara.

"But why not? I can hear him."

It's too soon for Jason, Sara. He's not asking yet. But he will. In time.

Now Sara understood more clearly why Jason and Billy

hadn't spotted Solomon yet. "They can't see you either, can they, Solomon?"

Sara was glad that Jason and Billy couldn't see Solomon. *They would really get in the way, if they could,* she thought.

Sara couldn't ever remember having a more wonderful time. She soared high into the sky, so high that the cars on Main Street looked like little ants moving about. And then, with what felt like no effort at all, she would swoop way down, very close to the ground, squealing as she felt the amazing speed of her flight. She swooped down right over the river with her face so close to the water that she could smell the sweet mossy scent, ducked right under the Main Street bridge, and then zoomed out the other side. Solomon kept perfect pace with her, as if they had practiced this flight hundreds of times.

They soared for what seemed like hours, and then, with the same powerful whoosh that sent Sara soaring upward, she was back in her body, and back on the ground.

Sara was so excited that she could barely catch her breath. This had truly been the most exceptional experience of her life. "Oh, Solomon, that was wonderful!" Sara squealed. It felt to her as if they had been flying for hours.

"What time is it?" Sara blurted, looking at her watch, certain that she would be in big trouble for being so tardy today, but her watch showed that only a few seconds had passed.

"Solomon, you live a very strange life, you know? Nothing is quite the way it's supposed to be."

What do you mean, Sara?

"Well, like, we can go flying all around town, and no time passes. Don't you find that strange? And like me being able to see you and talk to you, but Jason and Billy cannot see you or talk to you. Don't you find that strange?"

If their wanting were strong enough, they could, Sara, or if my wanting were strong enough, I could influence their wanting.

"What do you mean?"

It was their enthusiasm for something they hadn't actually seen that brought you to my thicket. They were a very important link in the unfolding of our meeting.

"Yeah, I guess." Sara didn't really want to give her little brother the credit for this extraordinary experience. She was more comfortable letting him keep his position as a thorn in her side. But a key to her joyful enlightenment?

That was too much of a stretch just yet.

So, Sara, tell me, what you have learned today? Solomon smiled.

"I've learned that I can fly all over town and no time will pass?" Sara stated questioningly, wondering if that was what Solomon wanted to hear. "I've learned that Jason and Billy can't hear me or see me when I fly, because they're too young, or not ready? I've learned that it isn't cold at all up there when you fly?"

*That is all very good, and we can talk all about that later, but, Sara, did you notice, that as long as you were talking about what you **didn't** want, that you couldn't get what you **did** want? But when you began talking about what you did want—even more important, when you were able to begin **feeling** what you did want—then it came instantly?*

Sara was quiet, trying to remember back. But it wasn't easy to think about anything that she was thinking or feeling before she was flying. She would much rather think about the flying part.

Sara, ponder this as often as you can, and practice it as much as you can.

"You want me to practice flying? All right!"

*Not just flying, Sara. **I want you to practice thinking about what you do want, and thinking about why you want what you want**—until you're able to really feel it. That is the most important thing you'll learn from me, Sara. Have fun with this.*

And with that, Solomon was up and away.

This is the best day of my life! Sara thought. *Today, I learned to fly!*

~~~
~~~

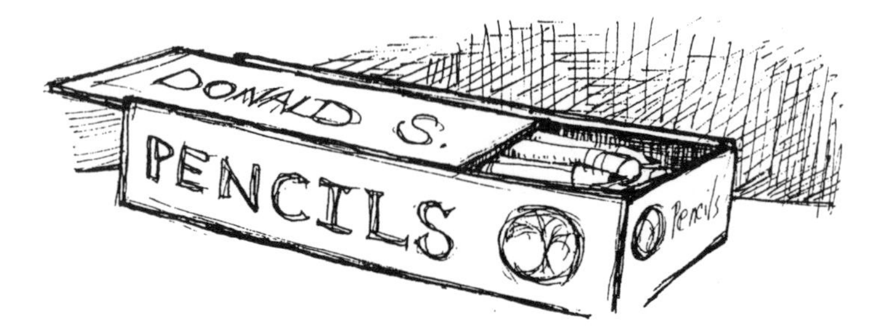

Chapter 10

"Hey, baby, do you still wet the bed at night?"

Sara felt angry as she watched them mocking Donald. Too shy to interfere, she tried to look away and not notice what was going on.

"They think they're so smart," Sara murmured under her breath. "They're just plain mean."

A couple "too cool to be alive" boys from her classroom, who were almost always seen together, were making fun of Donald, a new boy, who had only been in the classroom a couple of days. His family had just moved into town and was renting the old run-down house at the end of the street that Sara lived on. The house had been empty for months, and Sara's mother was happy to see someone finally moving in. Sara had noticed the rickety old truck being unloaded and had wondered if the little bit of broken-down furniture was really all that they had.

It's hard enough to be new in town and not know anyone, but to have these bullies picking on him already, well, that was just too much. Standing there in the hallway, watching Lynn and Tommy deliberately making Donald feel bad, Sara's eyes filled with tears. She remembered the outburst of laughter in her classroom yesterday when Donald was asked to stand to be introduced to his new classmates, and when he stood up he was clasping a bright red plastic pencil box. Sara admitted it wasn't the coolest thing to do—more appropriate for kids her little brother's age, but she certainly didn't believe that it deserved this kind of humiliation.

Sara realized that that had been the critical turning point for Donald. Had he been able to handle that first moment differently, perhaps standing bravely and grinning back, not caring what the rotten class thought about him, maybe things could have gotten off on a different foot. But that wasn't to be. For Donald, embarrassed and truly frightened, slumped into his chair, biting his lip. Sara's teacher had reprimanded the class, but that really made no difference at all. The class didn't seem to care what Mr. Jorgensen thought of them, but Donald surely did care what the class thought of him.

When he left the classroom yesterday, Sara had seen him drop his bright new pencil holder into the wastebasket by the door. Once Donald was out of sight, Sara had retrieved his ill-chosen trinket and had stuffed it into her school bag.

Sara watched as Tommy and Lynn went down the hallway. She listened to hear them clumping down the stairs. She could see Donald in front of his locker, just standing there, staring into it, as if there must be something in there that would make things better somehow, or as if he would like to crawl into the locker and avoid what was out here. Sara felt sick to her stomach. She didn't know what to do, but she wanted to do something to make Donald feel better. After looking down the hallway to make sure the bullies were really gone, she pulled the red box from her bag and hurried toward Donald, who was now fussing around with his books, in an ill-at-ease attempt to regain his composure.

"Hey, Donald, I saw you drop this yesterday," Sara said simply. "I think it's neat. I think you should keep it."

"No, I don't want it!" Donald snapped back.

Shocked, Sara stepped back and mentally tried to regain her balance.

"If you think it's so neat, you keep it!" Donald shouted at Sara.

Quickly stuffing it back into her bag, hoping no one had seen or heard this embarrassing exchange, Sara hurried into the school yard and headed home.

"Why don't I stay out of things?" Sara scolded herself. "Why don't I learn?"

CHAPTER 11

"Solomon, why are people so mean?" Sara pleaded.

Are all people mean, Sara? I hadn't noticed.

"Well, not all of them, but lots of them are, and I don't understand why. When I'm mean, I feel awful."

When are you mean, Sara?

"Mostly when someone is mean first. I think I sort of just get mean to pay them back."

Does that help?

"Yes," Sara offered defensively.

How so, Sara? Does paying them back make you feel better? Does it turn things around, or take any meanness back?

"Well, no, I guess not."

In fact, Sara, what I have seen is that it just adds more meanness to the world. It's a bit like joining their chain-of-pain. They are hurting, and then you're hurting, and then you help someone to hurt, and on and on it goes.

"But Solomon, who started this awful chain-of-pain?"

It doesn't really matter where it started, Sara. But it is *important what you do with it if it comes to you. What is this all about, Sara? What has caused you to join this chain-of-pain?*

Sara, feeling rather sick to her stomach, told Solomon about the new boy, Donald, and of his first day in class. She told Solomon about the bullies who seemed to find never-ending things to tease Donald about. She told Solomon about the alarming incident that had just taken place in the hallway. And as she relived what had happend, as she was describing them to Solomon she felt her painful anger growing again, and a tear pushed out of her eye and rolled down her cheek. She angrily wiped it away with the back of her sleeve, truly irritated that instead of her usual happy chatter with Solomon, she was now sniffling and blubbering. This wasn't the way it was supposed to be with Solomon.

Solomon was quiet for a long while as scattered, disconnected thoughts shot about Sara's mind. Sara could feel Solomon watching her with his big loving eyes, but she didn't feel self-conscious. It almost felt as if Solomon was drawing something out of her.

Well, it's clear what I ***don't*** *want,* Sara thought. *I don't want to feel like this. Especially when I'm talking with Solomon.*

That's very good, Sara. You have just, consciously, taken the first step in ending the chain-of-pain. You have consciously recognized what you ***do not*** *want.*

"And that's good?" Sara questioned. "It doesn't feel so good."

That's only because you have only taken the first step, Sara. There are three more.

"What is the next step, Solomon?"

Well, Sara, it isn't hard to figure out what you don't want. Do you agree with that?

"Yes, I guess I do. I mean, I think I usually know that."

How do you know that you're thinking about what you ***don't*** *want?*

"I can just sorta tell."

You can tell by the way you feel, Sara. When you're thinking about, or speaking about, something that you ***don't*** *want—you always feel negative emotion. You feel anger or disappointment or embarrassment or guilt or fear. You always feel bad when you're thinking about something you* ***don't*** *want.*

Sara thought back over the last few days, during which she had experienced more negative emotion than usual. "You're right, Solomon," Sara announced. "I've been feeling more of that this last week, watching those boys being mean to Donald. I've been so happy since meeting you, Solomon, and then so mad about them teasing Donald. I can see how the way I feel has to do with what I'm thinking about."

Good, Sara. Now, let's talk about step two. Whenever you know what you ***don't*** *want, isn't it rather easy to figure out what you* ***do*** *want?*

"Well . . ." Sara trailed off, wanting to understand, but still unsure.

When you're sick, what is it that you want?

"I want to feel better," Sara replied easily.

When you don't have enough money to buy something that you want, then what do you want?

"I want more money," Sara replied.

You see, Sara, that is step two of breaking the chain-of-pain. Step one is recognizing what you ***don't*** *want. Step two is then deciding what you* ***do*** *want.*

"Well, that's easy enough." Sara was beginning to feel better.

Step three is the most important step, Sara, and it's the step that most people miss altogether. Step three is this: Once you have identified what it is that you do want, you must make that feel real. You must talk about why you want it, describe what it would be like to have it, explain it, pretend it, or remember another time like it—but keep thinking about it until you find that feeling place. Continue to talk to yourself about what it is that you ***do*** *want until you* ***feel*** *good.*

As Sara listened to Solomon actually encouraging her to spend time, on purpose, imagining things in her own mind, she could hardly believe her ears. She'd gotten into serious trouble for that very thing on more than one occasion. It seemed that what Solomon was telling her was exactly opposite of what her teachers in school were telling her. But she had come to trust Solomon. And she was certainly willing to try something different. Their way, obviously, wasn't working.

"Why is step three the most important step, Solomon?"

Because, until you change the way you feel, you haven't really changed anything. You're still part of the chain-of-pain. But when you change the way you feel, you're part of a different chain. You have joined Solomon's chain, so to speak.

"What do you call your chain, Solomon?"

Well, I don't really call it anything. It's more about feeling it. But you might call it the Chain-of-Joy, or the Chain-of-Well-being. The Chain-of-Feeling-Good. It's the natural chain, Sara. It is truly who we all are.

"Well, if it's natural, if it's who we all are, why aren't more of us feeling good more of the time?"

People truly want to feel good, and most people want, very much, to be good. And that is a big part of the problem.

"What do you mean? How can wanting to be good be a problem?"

Well, Sara, people want to be good, so they look around them at the way others are living in order to decide what is good. They look at the conditions that surround them, and they see things that they believe are good, and they see things that they believe are bad.

"And that's bad? I don't see what's bad about that, Solomon."

What I've noticed, Sara, is that as they're looking at conditions, good ones and bad ones, most people aren't aware of how they are feeling. And that is what goes wrong for most of them. Rather than being aware of how what they are looking at is affecting them, in their quest for goodness, they keep searching out badness and trying to push that away. The trouble with that, Sara, is that the whole time they're trying to push away what they think is bad—they have joined the chain-of-pain. People are much more interested in looking at and analyzing and comparing conditions than they are aware of how they are feeling. And often the condition drags them right off into the chain-of-pain.

Sara, think back over the past few days, and try to remember some of the strong feelings that you had. What was happening as you were feeling bad this week, Sara?

"I felt awful when Tommy and Lynn were teasing Donald. I felt awful when the kids laughed at Donald in class, and I felt the very worst of all when Donald yelled at me. All I was trying to do was help him, Solomon."

Good, Sara. Let's talk about this. During those times that you were feeling so bad, what were you doing?

"I don't know, Solomon. I wasn't really doing anything. I was mostly just watching, I guess."

That is exactly right, Sara. You were observing conditions—but the conditions that you were choosing to observe were the kind that make you join the chain-of-pain.

"But Solomon," Sara argued, "how can you not see something that's wrong and not feel bad when you see it?"

That's a very good question, Sara, and I promise you that in time I will answer it fully for you. I know that it's not easy to understand this all at once. And the reason that it's difficult to understand at first is because you have been trained to observe conditions, but you have not been trained to pay attention to how you feel when you're observing—and so, the conditions seem to control your lives. If you're observing something good, you have a good feeling response, and if you're observing something bad, you have a bad feeling response. When the conditions seem to control your lives, that is frustrating for most of you, and that is what causes so many people to continue to join the chain-of-pain.

"Then, how can I stay out of the chain-of-pain so that I can help someone else out if they get in?"

Well, Sara, there are lots of ways to do that. But my favorite—the one that works the very fastest of all—is this: Think thoughts of appreciation.

"Appreciation?"

Yes, Sara, focus on something, or someone, and try to find thoughts that make you feel the very best. Appreciate them just as much as you can. That is the very best way to join the Chain-of-Joy.

Remember, step one is?

"Knowing what I *don't* want," Sara answered proudly. She had that one down pat.

And step two is?

"Knowing what I *do* want."

That's very good, Sara. And step three is?

"Oh, Solomon, I forget," Sara whined, disappointed at herself for forgetting so soon.

Step three is finding the feeling place of what you do want. *Talking about what you do want until you feel like you're already there.*

"Solomon, you never told me what step four is," Sara remembered, excitedly.

Ah, step four is the best part, Sara. That is when you get what you want. ***Step four is the physical manifestation of your desire.***

Have fun with this, Sara. Don't try too hard to remember all of this. ***Just practice appreciation. That's the key.*** *You'd better run along now, Sara. We can talk more about this tomorrow.*

Appreciation, Sara pondered. *I will try to think of things to appreciate.* Her little brother, Jason, was the first image that came to her mind. *Boy, this is going to be hard,* Sara thought, as she began walking from Solomon's thicket.

Start with something easier! Solomon called as he lifted from his post.

"Yeah, right." Sara laughed. *I love you, Solomon,* she thought.

I love you too, Sara. Sara heard Solomon's voice clearly, even though he had flown far from her view.

~~~
~~~

Chapter 12

Something easy, Sara thought, *I want to appreciate something easy.*

From a distance, Sara could see her next-door neighbor's dog frolicking in the snow. He was leaping and running, then rolling on his back, obviously happy to be alive.

Brownie, you're such a happy dog! I do appreciate you, Sara thought, still over 200 yards away. At that moment, Brownie began running toward Sara as if she were his master and had called his name. Wagging his tail, he ran two full circles around Sara, and then, with his paws on her shoulders, this large, mangy, long-haired dog pushed Sara into a sitting position into the pile of snow that was left by the snowplow earlier that week—and he licked her face with his warm, wet tongue. Sara was laughing so hard she could barely get up. "Oh, you love me, too, do you, Brownie?"

Sara lay in her bed that night thinking about everything that had happened that week. *I feel like I've been on a roller coaster. I've felt the best I have ever felt and the worst I have ever felt, all in one short week. I love my talks with Solomon, and, oh, how I loved learning to fly, but I got so mad this week, too. This is all very strange.*

Think thoughts of appreciation. Sara could have sworn she heard Solomon's voice in her bedroom.

"No, that cannot be," Sara decided. "I'm just remembering what Solomon said." And with that, Sara rolled over onto her side, to ponder. *I appreciate this nice warm bed, that's for sure,* Sara thought, as she tugged the blankets up over her shoulders. *And my pillow. My soft, snuggly pillow. I do appreciate this,* Sara thought, wrapping her arms around it and burying her face in it. *I appreciate my mother and my father. And Jas . . . and Jason, too.*

I don't know, Sara thought. *I don't think I'm finding that feeling place. Maybe I'm just too tired. I'll work on this tomorrow.* And with that last conscious thought, Sara was sound asleep.

"I'm flying again! I'm flying again!" Sara shouted, as she soared high above her house. *Flying isn't exactly the best word for this,* she thought. *More like floating. I can go anywhere I want to go!*

With no effort at all, but just by identifying where she wanted to be, Sara moved easily across the sky, pausing now and then to examine something she hadn't noticed before, sometimes swooping very close to the ground, and then lifting back up again. Up! Up! Up! She discovered that if she wanted to go down, all she had to do was stretch one toe toward the ground, and down she would go. When she was ready to go back up again, she just looked upward, and up she would go.

I want to fly forever and ever! Sara decided.

Let's see, Sara puzzled, *where should I go now?* Sara moved along, way up over her little town, seeing lights blinking off, here and there, as family after family, house after house, settled in for the night. It was beginning to snow very lightly, and Sara thrilled at how warm and secure she felt, floating about in the middle of the night in her bare feet and flannel nightgown. *It's not cold at all,* Sara noticed.

Nearly every house was dark now, and only the town's sparsely placed street lights were glowing, but on the far side of town, Sara could see one house still lit up. And so, she decided to go there to see who was still awake. *Probably somebody who doesn't have to get up early in the morning,* Sara thought, getting closer, and stretching her left toe downward, causing a perfect and rapid descent.

She dropped down to a small kitchen window, glad that the curtains were open so she could peek inside. And there, sitting at the kitchen table, with papers spread all over the place, was Mr. Jorgensen, Sara's teacher. Mr. Jorgensen was

methodically picking up one paper, reading it, then another, then another. Sara was transfixed as she watched him. He seemed to be so serious about whatever he was doing.

Sara began to feel a little bit guilty, spying on her teacher like this. *But at least this is the kitchen window,* Sara noted, *not the bathroom or bedroom, or something private like that.*

Now Mr. Jorgensen was smiling, seeming to really enjoy whatever he was reading. Now he was writing something on it. And then, suddenly, Sara realized what Mr. Jorgensen was doing. He was reading the papers Sara's class had turned in at the end of the day. He was reading every single one of them.

Sara had often found something scrawled on the top or the back of the papers he had returned to her, and she had never appreciated it much. *You just can't please him,* Sara had thought many times as she read his scribbled notes on her papers.

But watching this man, reading, then writing, reading and then writing, while almost everyone else in town was now fast asleep, left Sara feeling very strange. She felt almost dizzy as her old negative perspective of Mr. Jorgensen and her very new perspective of Mr. Jorgensen had a sort of collision inside her head. "Wow!" Sara said, as she looked upward, causing her little body to zoom up high above her teacher's house.

A warm gust of wind seemed to come from inside Sara, wrapping all around her body and giving her goose bumps on her skin. Her eyes filled with tears, and her heart leaped a happy beat and she soared, ever so high, into the sky, looking down upon her beautiful, sleeping, or almost-sleeping, town.

I feel appreciation for you, Mr. Jorgensen, Sara thought as she made one last swoop over his house and headed home. And as Sara looked back at Mr. Jorgensen's kitchen window, she felt sure that she saw him standing there, looking out.

CHAPTER 13

"Hi, Mr. Matson," Sara heard her own voice ring out as she crossed the Main Street bridge on her way to school.

Mr. Matson looked up from under the hood of the car he was working on. He had seen Sara on her way to school hundreds of mornings throughout the years that he had operated the town's one and only gas station on the corner of Main Street and Center Street, but she had never called out to him that way before. He really didn't know quite how to respond, so he waved a sort of half wave in his surprise. In fact, most people who knew Sara were beginning to notice startling differences in her usually introverted behavior. Instead of looking down, watching her feet, and being deep in her own thoughts, Sara was strangely interested in her mountain town, unusually observant and amazingly interactive.

"There are so many things to appreciate!" Sara was acknowledging quietly, under her breath. *The snowplow has already cleared most of the streets. That's really a nice thing,* Sara thought. *I do appreciate that.*

She saw a utility truck in front of Bergman's Store with its extension ladder extended all the way out. One man was at the very top of the ladder, working on a power pole, while another man watched intently from down below. Sara wondered what they were doing, and decided they were probably repairing one of the power lines that had become too heavy with icicles that were clinging to it. *That's really nice,* Sara thought. *It's so wonderful that these men are able to keep our electricity working. I do appreciate that.*

A school bus filled with children rounded the corner as Sara walked into the school yard. Sara couldn't see any of their faces because the windows were all fogged up, but she was very familiar with the routine: The bus driver, who had been gathering his unwilling cargo from all over the county since before dawn, was now releasing about half of them at Sara's school. He would unload the other half at Sara's old school down on Main Street. *That is a nice thing that the bus driver does,* Sara thought. *I really do appreciate that.*

Sara took off her heavy coat as she walked inside the school building, noticing how comfortably warm it felt inside. *I do appreciate this building, the furnace that keeps it warm, and the janitor who tends the furnace.* She remembered watching him shoveling chunks of coal into the bin that would feed the fire for a few more hours, and she had seen him removing the big red clinkers from the furnace. *I appreciate this janitor who does his job to keep us warm.*

Sara was feeling wonderful. *I'm really catching on to this appreciation stuff,* she thought. *I wonder why I hadn't figured this out sooner. This is great!*

"Hey, Baby Face!" Sara heard a contrived whiny voice taunting someone. The words felt so awful that Sara winced as she heard them. It was shocking to come from a place of feeling soooo wonderful to this sickening realization that someone was picking on someone.

Oh, no, Sara thought, *not Donald again.* But sure enough, the same two bullies were at it again. They had Donald cornered in the hallway. His body was pressed up against his locker, and Sara could see Lynn's and Tommy's grinning faces only inches from his.

Suddenly, Sara wasn't shy at all. "Why don't you goons find someone your own size to pick on?" Well, that wasn't exactly what Sara meant to say, since Donald was actually quite a bit taller than either of them, but the confidence that they seemed to gather from always running in packs, left Donald, or whoever they were picking on at the moment, at a seeming disadvantage.

"Oh, Donald's got a girlfriend, Donald's got a girlfriend," the boys chanted in unison. Sara's face flushed red with embarrassment and then redder with anger.

The boys laughed and moved on down the hallway, leaving Sara standing there, flushed and feeling very hot and uncomfortable.

"I don't need you to stick up for me!" Donald shouted, again blasting Sara to conceal his tears of embarrassment.

Good grief, Sara thought. *I'm doing it again. I just don't learn.*

Well, Donald, Sara thought, *I appreciate you, too. You have, once again, helped me to realize that I am an idiot. An idiot who does not learn.*

~~~

~~~

CHAPTER 14

"Hi, Solomon," Sara offered flatly, hanging her book bag over the post next to the owl's post.

Good day, Sara. It's a beautiful day. Do you agree?

"Yes, I guess it is." Sara replied blankly, not really noticing, or even caring, that the sun was shining brightly again. Sara loosened her neck scarf and tugged it from around her neck, stuffing it into her pocket.

Solomon waited quietly for Sara to gather her thoughts and begin her usual barrage of questions, but Sara was unusually sullen today.

"Solomon," Sara began, "I don't get it."

What is it that you do not understand, Sara?

"I don't understand what good it does anybody for me to go around appreciating things. I mean, I really don't see what good it's doing."

What do you mean, Sara?

"Well, I mean, I was getting pretty good at it. I've been practicing it all week. At first it was pretty hard, but then it got easier. And today, I was appreciating just about everything until I got to school and heard Lynn and Tommy picking on poor Donald, again."

Then what happened?

"Then I got mad. I got so mad I yelled at them. I just wanted them to leave Donald alone so that he can be happy. But I did it again, Solomon. I joined their chain-of-pain. I haven't learned anything. I just hate those boys, Solomon. I think they're awful."

Why do you hate them?

"Because they ruined my perfect day. Today I was going to appreciate things. When I woke up this morning, I appreciated my bed and then my breakfast, and my mother and father, and even Jason. And all the way to school I found so many things to appreciate, and then they ruined it, Solomon. They made me feel awful again. Like before. Just like before I learned how to appreciate."

It's no wonder you're mad at them, Sara, for you're in a terrible trap. In fact, that is just about the worst trap in the world.

Sara didn't much like the sound of that. She'd seen enough of Jason and Billy's homemade traps, and had freed many little mice and squirrels and birds that they had gleefully captured. The idea of someone putting her in a trap made Sara feel awful. "What do you mean, Solomon? What trap?"

Well, Sara, when your happiness depends on what somebody else does or does not do, you're trapped, because you cannot control what they think or what they do. But, Sara, you will discover true liberation—a freedom beyond your wildest dreams—when you discover that your joy does not depend on anyone else. Your joy only depends on what **you** *choose to give your attention to.*

Sara listened quietly with tears running down her pink cheeks.

You feel trapped right now because you don't see how you could respond differently to what you saw happen. As you witness something that makes you feel uncomfortable, you're responding to those conditions. And you think that the only way you can feel better is if the conditions are better. And since you cannot control the conditions, you feel trapped.

Sara wiped her face with her sleeve. She felt very

uncomfortable. Solomon was right. She did feel trapped. And she wanted to be free of the trap.

Sara, just keep working on appreciating—and you'll begin to feel better. We'll sort this out a little bit at a time. You'll see. This will not be difficult for you to understand. Keep having fun. We'll talk more tomorrow. Sleep well.

~~~

~~~

Chapter 15

Solomon was right. Things did seem to just get better and better. In fact, the next few weeks were the best that Sara could ever remember. Everything seemed to be going so well. The school days seemed to be getting shorter and shorter, and to Sara's surprise, she was actually beginning to like school. But Solomon continued to be the very best part of Sara's day.

"Solomon," Sara said, "I'm so glad that I found you here in this thicket. You're my best friend."

I'm glad, too, Sara. We are birds of a feather, you know?

"Well, you're half right, anyway," Sara laughed, looking at Solomon's beautiful coat of feathers and feeling that warm wind of appreciation flowing through her. She had heard her mother say, "Birds of a feather flock together," but she had never thought much about what it meant, and she certainly never expected that she would ever find herself flocking with birds.

"What does that mean, anyway, Solomon?"

People use that expression to point out their awareness that things that are like one another come together. That which is like unto itself is drawn.

"You mean, like robins stay together, and crows stay together, and squirrels stay together?"

Well, yes, like that. But really, all things that are alike do that, Sara. But the likeness is not always what you think it is. It is not usually something obvious that you can see.

"I don't understand, Solomon. If you can't see it, how do you know that they are alike or different?"

You can feel it, Sara. But it takes practice, and before you can practice, you have to know what you're looking for, and since most people don't understand the basic rules, they don't know what to look for.

"Rules, like in rules of a game, Solomon?"

Yes, sort of like that. Actually, a better name would be 'the Law of Attraction.' ***The Law of Attraction says: 'That which is like unto itself is drawn.'***

"Oh, I see." Sara brightened. "Like birds of a feather flock together."

That's it, Sara. And everyone and everything in the entire Universe is affected by this Law.

"I still don't really understand this, Solomon. Tell me more, please."

Tomorrow, as you're moving through your day, watch for the evidence of this Law. Keep your eyes and ears open, and, most important, pay attention to the way that you feel as you observe things and people and animals and situations around you. Have fun with this, Sara. We'll talk more about it tomorrow.

Hmm, birds of a feather, flock together, Sara pondered. And as those words rolled across her mind, a large flock of geese flushed up from the pasture and flapped above Sara's head. Sara had always loved watching these winter geese, and she was always amazed by the patterns they made as they flew across the sky. Sara laughed at the seeming coincidence of talking about flocking birds and then immediately finding the sky filled with them. *Hmm, the Law of Attraction!*

~~~

~~~

CHAPTER 16

Mr. Pack's shiny old Buick slowed down as it passed Sara. She waved at Mr. and Mrs. Pack, and they smiled and waved back.

Sara remembered her father's comments about their elderly neighbors. "Those old geezers are just alike."

"They even seem to look alike," her mother had added.

Hmm, Sara pondered, *they are very much alike.* Sara thought back over the time she had known these neighbors. "They are both as neat as a button," her mother had noticed right from the beginning. Mr. Pack's car was always the shiniest in town. "He must wash it every day," Sara's father had groaned, not appreciating the contrast that Mr. Pack's, always clean car struck with his own usually dirty one. Mr. Pack's summer lawn and gardens were always trimmed and planted to perfection, and Mrs. Pack was every bit as tidy as her husband. Sara didn't have much opportunity to be inside their house, but on the rare occasion that she had run an errand for her mother that had taken her inside, Sara was always impressed with the house, always tidy and clean, never even one thing out of place. *Ah, the Law of Attraction,* Sara concluded.

Sara's brother, Jason, and his rambunctious friend, Billy, sped by Sara on their bicycles, each coming as close to Sara as possible without actually bumping her. "Hey, Sara, better watch where you're going," Jason chided. Sara could hear them laughing as they raced down the road.

Brats! Sara thought, as she reclaimed her place back on the roadway, irritated that she had scrambled to get out of their way. "They were made for each other," Sara grumbled. "They take such delight in making trouble." Sara stopped dead in her tracks. "Birds of a feather." Sara brightened. "They are birds of a feather! This is the Law of Attraction!"

And everyone and everything in the Universe is affected by it! Sara remembered Solomon's words.

The next day, Sara spent as much time as possible looking for evidence of the Law of Attraction.

It's everywhere! Sara concluded, as she observed adults, children, and teenagers moving about her town.

Sara stopped at Hoyt's Store, a sort of general store right in the middle of town and only slightly out of Sara's way to school. She bought a new eraser to replace the one someone had borrowed yesterday and had not returned, and a candy bar to eat after lunch.

Sara had always liked coming into this store. It always felt good. The store was owned by three cheerful men who were always ready and willing to play with whoever walked into the store. It was always a very busy place, since it was the only grocery store in town, but even when the lines were long, these three men managed to joke and kid with anyone who was willing to play along.

"How's it going, Kiddo?" the taller of the three quipped at Sara.

His enthusiasm startled Sara a bit. They had never played much with Sara, which had always suited Sara just fine, but today, they clearly intended to make Sara part of their fun.

"It's going fine," Sara replied boldly.

"Well, that's what I like to hear! Which are you going to eat first, the candy bar or the eraser?"

"I thought I'd eat the candy bar first. I'll save the eraser for dessert!" Sara grinned back at him.

Mr. Hoyt laughed hard. Sara had truly taken him off guard with her quick humor. Sara's clever reply had surprised Sara, too.

"Well, you have a good day, sweetheart! Keep having fun!"

Sara felt wonderful as she walked back out onto Main Street. *Birds of a feather,* Sara pondered. *The Law of Attraction. It's everywhere!*

What a beautiful day! Sara appreciated just leaning back, looking upward at the bright blue sky on this exceptionally warm winter day. The usually frozen streets and sidewalks were shining wet, and little streams of water were trickling across Sara's path, forming little puddles here and there.

"Varooooom!" Jason and Billy yelled in unison as they whizzed past Sara, riding their bicycles as fast and as close to her as they could without bumping into her. Dirty water splashed up Sara's legs.

"Monsters!" Sara yelled, dripping with muddy water and seething with anger. *This just doesn't make sense. I've got to ask Solomon about this.*

Her wet clothes dried and most of the muddy marks were brushed away, but by the end of the day Sara was still confused and angry. She was mad at Jason, but then there wasn't anything new in that. Sara felt angry at Solomon, too, and at the Law of Attraction and Birds of a Feather and at mean people. In fact, Sara was pretty much mad at everybody.

As always, Solomon was perched on his post, waiting patiently for Sara's visit.

You seem unusually excited today, Sara. What is it you'd like to talk about?

"Solomon!" Sara blurted, "Something is really wrong with this Law of Attraction thing!"

Sara waited, expecting Solomon to correct her.

Go on, Sara.

"Well, you said that the Law of Attraction says that that which is like unto itself is drawn? And Jason and Billy are really rotten, Solomon. They spend all day, mostly, looking for ways to make other people feel bad." Sara paused a bit, still expecting Solomon to interrupt.

Go on.

"Well, Solomon, I'm not rotten. I mean, I don't splash mud on people or bump them with my bicycle. I don't trap or kill little animals or let the air out of people's tires, so how come Jason and Billy keep flocking with me? We aren't birds of a feather, Solomon. We are different!"

Do you think that Jason and Billy are truly rotten, Sara?

"Yes, Solomon, I do!"

They are rascals, I'll agree with you there, Solomon nodded, *but they are pretty much like everyone and everything in the Universe. They have that which is wanted, and the lack of it, all mixed in together. Have you ever noticed your brother doing something nice?*

"Well, yes, I guess. But hardly ever," Sara stammered. "I'd have to think about that. But Solomon, I still don't get it. Why do they keep bothering me? I don't bother them!"

Well, Sara, this is the way it works. In every moment, you have the option of looking at something that you want, or at the lack of it. When you're looking at something you want—just by observing it, you begin to vibrate as it is. You become the same as it is, Sara. Do you understand?

"You mean that just by watching someone who is rotten, I'm rotten, too?"

Well, not exactly, but you're beginning to understand. Imagine a light board, about the size of your bed.

"A light board?"

*Yes, Sara. A board with thousands of little lights, like little Christmas tree lights, protruding up from the board. A sea of lights. Thousands of them, and you're one of these lights. When you give your attention to something, just by giving it your attention, your light on the board lights up, and, in that moment, every other light on the board—**that is in vibrational harmony with your light**—lights up, too. And those lights represent your world. Those are the people and experiences that you now have vibrational access to.*

Think about it, Sara. Of all the people you know, who does your brother, Jason, tease and harass the most?

Sara answered instantly. "Me, Solomon. He's always bothering me!"

And of all the people you know, who do you think is most bothered by Jason's teasing? Who do you think lights their light board in vibrational harmony with these rascals, Sara?

Sara laughed, now beginning to understand. "It's me,

Solomon. I am most bothered. I keep lighting my light board by watching Jason and getting mad at him."

So you see, Sara, as you see something you do not like, and you notice it and push against it and think about it—you light your light board, and then you get more of that. Often, you're vibrating there even when Jason is nowhere around. You're just remembering the last thing that happened when he ***was*** *around. The nice thing about all of this, Sara, is this: You can always tell, by the way you're feeling, what you're achieving vibrational harmony with.*

"What do you mean?"

Whenever you're happy, whenever you're feeling appreciation, whenever you're noticing the positive aspects of someone or something, you're vibrating in harmony with what you ***do*** *want. But whenever you feel angry or fearful, whenever you feel guilty or disappointed, you're—in that very moment—achieving harmony with what you* ***don't*** *want.*

"Every single time, Solomon?"

Yes. Every time. You can always trust the way you feel. It's your Guidance System. Ponder this, Sara. In the next few days, as you're observing those around you, pay particular attention to the way you're feeling. Show yourself, Sara, what ***you*** *are achieving vibrational harmony with.*

"Okay, Solomon. I'll try. But this is pretty tricky, you know. This may take a lot of practice."

Agreed. It's nice that there are so many others around you to give you an opportunity to practice. Have fun with this.

And with that, Solomon was up and away.

Easy for you to say, Solomon, Sara thought. *You get to choose who you spend time with. You're not stuck in school with Lynn and Tommy. You don't have to live with Jason.*

Then, as clearly as if Solomon were sitting right there speaking directly into Sara's ears, she heard: *When your happiness depends on what somebody else does or does not do, you're trapped, because you cannot control what they think or what they do. You will discover a true liberation, a freedom beyond your wildest dreams, when you discover that your joy does not depend on anyone else.* ***Your joy only depends on what you choose to give your attention to.***

Chapter 17

W*hat a day this has been,* Sara thought as she walked toward Solomon's thicket.

"I hate school!" Sara blurted out loud as she slipped back into the feeling of anger that had begun the very moment she had walked onto the school grounds. She walked along, looking mostly down at her feet, recalling the details of this wretched day.

She had arrived at the front gate at the same moment that the school bus arrived, and when the bus driver opened the doors, a herd of rowdy boys had almost mowed Sara down, bumping her from every direction, causing her to drop her books, spilling the contents of her bag. And worst of all, her theme paper for Mr. Jorgensen had been literally trampled. Sara gathered the crumpled, muddied papers into a pile and stuffed them into her bag. "That's what I get for caring what the stupid paper looks like," Sara had grumbled, now regretting having taken the time to rewrite it a second time before folding it carefully and putting it into her book bag.

Still trying to get things back together as she walked through the big front doors, Sara wasn't moving fast enough for Miss Webster. "Move along, Sara, I don't have all day!" the slender, and mostly hated, third-grade teacher had snapped at Sara.

"Excuse me for being alive!" Sara had muttered under her breath. "Good grief!"

Sara must have looked at her watch 100 times during the day, counting the minutes to some freedom from this rampage of meanness.

And then, at last, the final bell rang, and Sara was free.

"I hate school. I really hate school. How can something that feels so terrible be of any value to anyone?"

Out of habit, Sara made her way to Solomon's thicket, and as she made the last turn onto Thacker's Trail, Sara thought, *This is the very worst mood I've been in ever. Especially since meeting Solomon.*

"Solomon," Sara complained, "I hate school. I think it's a waste of time."

Solomon was very quiet.

"It's like a cage that you can't get out of, and the people in the cage are mean and are looking for ways to hurt you all day long."

Still no comment from Solomon.

"It's bad enough when the kids are mean to each other, but the teachers are mean, too, Solomon. I don't think they like being there either."

Solomon just sat there staring. Only the occasional blinking of his big yellow eyes let Sara know that he wasn't sound asleep.

A tear slipped down Sara's cheek as her frustration welled up within her. "Solomon, I just want to be happy. And I don't think I will ever be happy at school."

Well then, Sara, I think you'd better get out of town, too.

Sara looked up, startled by Solomon's sudden comment.

"What did you say, Solomon? Get out of town, too?"

Yes, Sara, if you're leaving your school because there are some negative things there, then I think you should get out of town, too, and out of this state and out of this country and off the face of this Earth, even out of this Universe. And now, Sara, I don't know where to send you.

Sara was confused. This didn't seem like the solution-seeking Solomon she had come to know and love.

"Solomon, what are you saying?"

Well, Sara, I've discovered that in every single particle of the Universe there is that which is wanted and the lack of it. In every person, in every situation, in every place, in every moment—those choices are always there. Ever present. So you see, Sara, if you're leaving one place or circumstance because there is negative in it, the next place you go will be pretty much the same.

"You're not making me feel better, Solomon. It feels hopeless."

Sara, your work is not to look for the perfect place where only the things you want exist. Your work is to look for the things you want in ***every*** *place.*

"But why? What good does that do?"

Well, for one thing, you would feel better, and, for another thing, ***as you begin to notice more things that you want to see, more of those things begin to become part of your experience.*** *It gets easier and easier, Sara.*

"But, Solomon, aren't some places a lot worse than others? I mean school is just the worst place in the world to be."

Well, Sara, it's easier to find positive things in some places than others, but that can become a pretty big trap.

"What do you mean?"

When you see something you don't like and you decide to go somewhere else to get away from it, you usually take it with you.

"But Solomon, I wouldn't take those mean teachers or rotten kids with me."

Well, maybe not those very same ones, Sara, but you would meet others, very much like them, everywhere you would go. Sara, remember "Birds of a Feather." Remember the "Light Board." When you see things you don't like and you think about them and talk about them, you become like them, and then everywhere you go, they are there, too.

"Solomon, I keep forgetting all of this."

Well, Sara, it's natural to forget this, because you're like most people who have learned to respond to conditions. If good conditions are around you, you respond by feeling good, but if there are bad conditions around you, you respond by feeling bad.

Most people think that they must first find perfect conditions, and once they find those perfect conditions, then they can respond by being happy. But that is very frustrating to people, because they discover, very soon, that they cannot control the conditions.

What you're learning, Sara, is that you aren't here to find perfect conditions. You're here to choose things to appreciate—which causes you to vibrate like the perfect conditions—so that you can then attract perfect conditions.

"I guess," Sara sighed. This all seemed too big to understand.

Sara, it really isn't as complicated as it seems. In fact, people make it much more complicated as they try to make sense of all of the conditions that surround them. It can get very confusing if you're trying to figure out how every condition is created, or which conditions are right and which ones are wrong. You can drive yourself crazy trying to sort all of that out. But if you will just pay attention to whether your valve is open or closed, then your life will be much simpler and much happier.

"My valve? What do you mean?"

Sara, in every moment, a stream of pure, positive energy is flowing to you. You might say it's a bit like the water pressure in your house. That water pressure is always there, right up against your valve. And when you want water in your house, you open the valve and let the water flow in. But when the valve is closed shut, the water doesn't flow in. It's your work to keep this valve to Well-

being open. It's always there for you, but you must let it in.

"But Solomon," Sara protested, "what good does it do for me to keep my valve open in a school where everyone else is angry and mean?"

First of all, when your valve is open, you won't notice so much of the meanness, and some of it will change right before your eyes. There are many people who are sort of teetering on the edge of an open or closed valve, and when they come into contact with you and your valve is wide open, they easily join you in a smile, or a nice interchange. Also, you must remember that an open valve is not only affecting what is happening right now. It's affecting tomorrow and the next day. So, the more todays that you're feeling good, the more conditions of tomorrow and the next day will be pleasing to you. Practice this, Sara.

Make a decision that no condition, no matter how bad it may seem to you in the moment, is worth your closing your valve. Decide that keeping your valve open is the most important thing.

Here are some words to remember, Sara, and to say, as often as you can: "I am going to keep my valve open anyway."

"Well, all right, Solomon," Sara replied meekly, feeling

tentative about the whole thing, but remembering how much better things, on the whole, had been going since she had tried some of the other techniques Solomon had offered.

"I'll practice this. I hope it works," Sara called back over her shoulder as she left Solomon's thicket. *It would certainly be nice to be able to feel good no matter what. That really is what I want.*

~~~
~~~

Chapter 18

Sara's mother's car was in the driveway. *That's strange,* Sara thought. *She's not supposed to be home this early.*

"Hi, I'm home," Sara called out, as she opened the front door, surprising herself with such an unusual announcement of her arrival. But no answer came back. Sara put her books down on the dining room table and called again, walking through the kitchen into the hallway leading to the bedrooms, "Anybody home?"

"I'm in here, honey," Sara heard her mother's quiet voice. The drapes in her mother's bedroom were closed, and Sara's mom was lying on her bed with a pink rolled towel across her eyes and forehead.

"What's wrong, Mom?" Sara asked.

"Oh, I just have a headache, honey. It's been hurting all day, and finally I decided I couldn't stay at work another minute, so I came home."

"Is it better now?"

"It feels better to have my eyes closed. I'll just lie here for a little while. I'll be out later. Close the door for me, and when your brother comes home, tell him I'll be out later. Maybe if I can sleep for a little while, I'll feel better."

Sara tiptoed out of the room and gently closed the door. She stood in the dark hallway for a bit, trying to decide what to do next. She knew what chores should be tended to, as she had done those same chores every day for as long as she could remember, but everything felt different somehow.

Sara couldn't remember the last time her mother had stayed home from work, sick, and there was something very unsettling about all of this. Sara had a knot in her stomach and she felt disoriented. She hadn't realized how her mother's usual stability and good humor had such a stabilizing influence on her own day.

"I don't like this," Sara said aloud. "I hope Mom feels better, fast."

Sara. Sara heard Solomon's voice. *Does your happiness depend on the conditions around you? This might be a good opportunity to practice.*

"Okay, Solomon. But how do I practice? What am I supposed to do?"

Just open your valve, Sara. When you feel bad, your valve is closed. So try to think thoughts that feel better until you feel your valve open up again.

Sara went out into the kitchen, but her thoughts were still mostly about her mother lying in her bed in the next room. Her mother's purse was on the kitchen table, so Sara couldn't stop thinking about her.

Make a decision to do something, Sara. Think about your chores, and decide to do them in record time tonight. Think about doing something extra, something beyond your normal chores.

And with that idea, Sara was inspired to instant action. She moved quickly and certainly, picking up things from around the house that had been misplaced slowly, over many hours last evening before bedtime, by various members of the family. She gathered and stacked the newspapers that seemed to cover most of the living room floor, and then dusted the table tops in the living room. She cleaned the sink and the bathtub in the family's only bathroom. She emptied the garbage cans from the kitchen and the bathroom. She tidied the papers strewn across her father's great big oak desk, which was awkwardly crammed in the corner of the living room, being careful not to move anything too far from where her father had placed it.

She was never certain if there was order to his disorder, but she didn't want to cause any problems. Her father actually spent very little time at that desk, and Sara often wondered why such a big piece of the living room had to be devoted to it. But it seemed to give her father a place to think, and, more important, a place to stash things he didn't want to think about right now.

She was moving quickly, with strong, decisive purpose, and it wasn't until she made the decision not to use the vacuum cleaner on the living room carpet, because she didn't want to disturb her mother, that she realized how good she had come to feel in such a short time. But, in deciding not to vacuum, and perhaps disturb her resting mother, her attention was drawn back to the negative condition; and that dull, icky feeling came back into her stomach.

Wow! Sara pondered. *That's amazing. I can actually see that the way I feel has only to do with what I'm giving my attention to. The conditions didn't change, but my attention did!*

Sara felt elated. She realized something very important. She had discovered that her joy is truly not dependent on anyone or anything else.

Then Sara heard her mother's bedroom door open, and her mom emerged from the hallway into the kitchen. "Oh, Sara, everything looks so nice!" her mother exclaimed, obviously feeling much better.

"Did your headache go away, Mom?" Sara asked tenderly.

"It's much better now, Sara. I was able to rest for a while because I could tell you were out here taking care of things. Thank you, sweetheart."

Sara felt wonderful. She knew that she hadn't actually *done* much more than she did every single day after school. Her mother wasn't appreciating Sara for her action. Her mother was appreciative of Sara's open valve. *I can do this,* Sara decided. *I can keep my valve open no matter the conditions.*

Sara remembered Solomon's affirmation: *I will keep my valve open—anyway!*

~~~

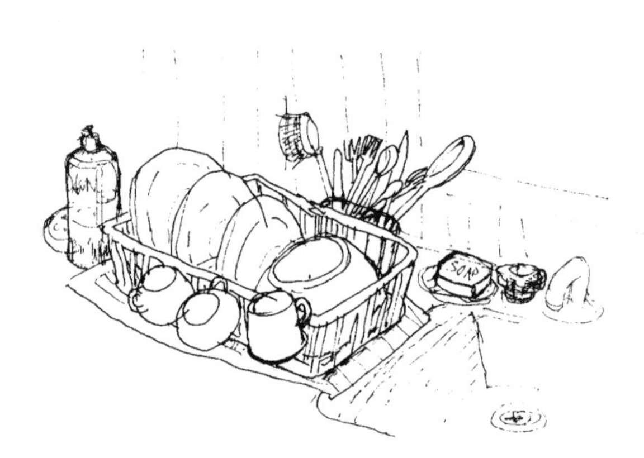
~~~

Chapter 19

Very nice, Sara—an A. Sara read the words scrawled across the top of yesterday's assignment, just handed back to her by Mr. Jorgensen.

Sara tried to stifle an ear-to-ear grin as she read the words written in bright red ink. Mr. Jorgensen glanced back at Sara as he handed the girl in front of her her paper, and when Sara's eyes met his, he winked at her.

Sara felt her heart jump. She felt very proud. This was a new feeling for Sara, and one, she noticed, that she liked very much.

Sara couldn't wait to get to the thicket to talk to Solomon.

"Solomon, what has happened to Mr. Jorgensen?" Sara asked. "He seems like a different man."

He's the same man, Sara; you're just noticing different things.

"I don't think I'm noticing different things; I think he's doing different things."

Like what, Sara?

"Well, like he smiles a lot more than he used to. And sometimes he whistles before the bell rings. He never used to do that. He even winked at me! And he's been telling better stories in class, making the class laugh more. Solomon, he just seems a whole lot happier than he used to."

Well, Sara. It sounds like your teacher may have joined your chain-of-joy.

Sara was stunned. Was Solomon actually trying to give Sara the credit for Mr. Jorgensen's change in behavior?

"Solomon, are you saying that I made Mr. Jorgensen happier?"

Well, it's not only your doing, Sara, because Mr. Jorgensen truly wants to be happy. But you did help him to remember that he wants to be happy. And you did help him to remember why he decided to become a teacher to begin with.

"But Solomon, I haven't talked to Mr. Jorgensen about any of that. How could I have helped him to remember that?"

You did all of that, Sara, with your appreciation of Mr. Jorgensen. You see, anytime you hold someone, or something, as your object of attention, and at the same time, you're feeling that wonderful feeling of appreciation—you add to their state of Well-being. You shower them with your appreciation.

"Like spraying them with the garden hose?" Sara giggled, pleased with her own silly analogy.

Yes, Sara. it's very much like that. But before you can actually spray them, you have to hook your hose to the faucet and turn it on. And that is what the appreciation does. Whenever you're feeling appreciation or love, whenever you're seeing something positive about someone or something, you're hooked to the faucet.

"Who puts the appreciation in the faucet, Solomon? Where does it come from?"

It has always been there, Sara. It's just naturally there.

"Well, then, why aren't more people spraying it around?"

Well, because most people have disconnected from the faucet, Sara. Not intentionally, but they just don't understand how to stay connected.

"Okay, then, Solomon, are you saying that I can hook up to it anytime that I want to and I can spray it around, anyplace, anytime, on anything I want to?"

That's right, Sara. And wherever you spray your hose of appreciation, you will begin to notice very obvious changes.

"Wow!" Sara whispered, mentally trying to size up the magnitude of what she had just learned. "Solomon, this is like magic!"

It seems like magic at first, Sara, but in time it begins to feel very natural. Feeling good—and then being a catalyst to help others feel good—is the most natural thing you will ever do!

Sara gathered her book bag and her discarded jacket, getting ready to tell Solomon good-bye for this day.

Just remember, Sara, your work is to stay hooked to the faucet.

Sara stopped and turned back to Solomon, realizing, suddenly, that this may not be as easy or as magical as Solomon had made it sound at first.

"Is there a trick to that, Solomon, to stay hooked to the faucet?"

It may take a little practice at first. You'll get better and better at it. For the next few days, just think about something, and then pay attention to how you feel. You'll notice, Sara, that when you're appreciating or basking or applauding or seeing positive aspects, you'll feel wonderful, and that means you're hooked to the faucet. But when you're blaming or criticizing or finding fault, you won't feel good. And that means you're unhooked, at least for the time you're feeling bad. Have fun with this, Sara. And with those last words, Solomon was gone.

Sara felt such exhilaration as she walked home that day. She had already enjoyed Solomon's game of appreciation, but the idea of appreciating with the intent of hooking to this wonderful faucet excited her even more. Somehow it gave Sara more reason to appreciate.

Sara rounded the corner for the last stretch of her walk home and saw Old Aunt Zoie moving very slowly up her walkway. All winter long, Sara hadn't seen her at all, and she was surprised to see her outside. Aunt Zoie didn't see Sara, so Sara didn't call out to her, not wanting to startle her, and also, not wanting to get involved in the long

conversation that was probable. Aunt Zoie talked very slowly, and over the years, Sara had learned to avoid the frustration of seeing her groping for words to express her thoughts. It was as if her mind worked so much faster than her mouth that she would get all mixed up about where she was within the thought. When Sara tried to help by putting a word in here and there, it only irritated Aunt Zoie. So Sara had decided that avoidance was the best solution—although that never really felt right either. Sara felt sad as she watched this poor old woman hobbling up her stairs. She was holding on to the railing with all of her strength, taking one step at a time, very slowly moving up a set of four or five stairs onto her front porch.

I hope I'm not like that when I'm old, Sara thought. And then Sara remembered her last talk with Solomon. *The faucet! I'll shower her with the faucet! First, I connect to the faucet, and then I flow it all over her.* But the feeling wasn't there. *Okay, I'll try again.* Still, no feeling of being hooked up. Sara felt instant frustration. "But Solomon," she pleaded, "this is really important. Aunt Zoie needs to be sprayed." No reply from Solomon. "Solomon, where are you?" Sara shouted out loud, not even realizing Aunt Zoie had now noticed her and was standing at the top of the stairs watching her.

"Who are you talking to?" Aunt Zoie barked.

Sara was startled and embarrassed. "Oh, nobody," she replied. And she scampered quickly down the path, past Aunt Zoie's garden, now just a muddy field waiting for the new spring planting. Red-faced and angry, Sara went home.

~~~
~~~

Chapter 20

"Solomon, where were you yesterday?" Sara whined, as she encountered Solomon on his post. "I needed you to help me hook to the faucet so that I could help Aunt Zoie feel better."

Do you understand why you were having trouble hooking up, Sara?

"No, Solomon. Why couldn't I hook up? I really wanted to."

Why?

"I really wanted to help Aunt Zoie. She is so old and confused. Her life just can't be much fun."

And so you wanted to hook to the flow, to shower Aunt Zoie, to fix what is wrong with her, so that she can be happy?

"Yes, Solomon. Will you help me?"

Well, Sara, I would like to help you, but I'm afraid that it's not possible.

"Why not, Solomon? What do you mean? She is really the nicest old lady. You'd like her, I think. I'm sure she has never done anything wrong . . ."

Sara, I'm sure you're right. Aunt Zoie is a wonderful woman. The reason we can't help her, under these circumstances, has nothing to do with her; it's you, Sara.

"Me?! What did I do, Solomon? I'm just trying to help her!"

Yes, indeed, Sara. That is what you're wanting. It's just that you're going about it in a way that cannot work. Remember, Sara, your work is to connect to the faucet.

"I know that, Solomon. That's why I needed you. To help me hook up."

But you see, Sara, I can't help you either. ***You*** *have to find that feeling place.*

"Solomon, I don't get it."

Remember, Sara, you cannot be part of the chain-of-pain and hooked to the faucet of Well-being at the same time. It's one or the other. When you're observing an unwanted condition that causes you to feel bad, that bad feeling is how you know you're unhooked. And when you're not connected to the natural flow of Well-being, you have nothing to give to another.

"Good grief, Solomon, it seems impossible. If I see someone who needs help, just seeing them needing help makes me vibrate in a way that I can't help them. That's just awful. How can I ever help anybody?"

You have to remember that the most important thing is to stay connected to the faucet of Well-being so you must hold your thoughts in a position that keeps you feeling good. In other words, Sara, you have to be more aware of your connection to the faucet of Well-being than you're aware of the conditions. That's the key.

Sara, think back about what happened yesterday. Tell me what happened with Aunt Zoie.

"Okay. I was walking home from school, and I saw Aunt Zoie hobbling up her front sidewalk. She's all crippled, Solomon. She can hardly walk at all. She has this old cane made out of real old wood that she uses to hold herself up."

And then what happened?

"Well, nothing really happened. I was just thinking how sad it is that she is so crippled . . ."

And then what happened?

"Well, nothing happened, Solomon . . ."

How were you feeling about then, Sara?

"Well, Solomon, I felt real bad. I felt really sorry for Aunt Zoie. She could hardly pull herself up the steps. And then I felt scared that I might be like that when I get old, too."

Now that is the most important point in this whole thing, Sara. When you notice that you're feeling bad, that's how you know that you're looking at a condition that disconnects you from the faucet. You see, Sara, in truth, you're naturally hooked to the faucet. You don't have to work to get hooked to it. But it's important to pay attention to how you're feeling so you know when you're ***unhooked****. That's what negative emotion is.*

"But what should I have done to stay hooked up, Solomon?"

I have noticed, Sara, that when it's your top priority to stay hooked, you find more and more thoughts that keep you hooked up. But until you truly understand that that is what is most important, most of you will go off on all kinds of wild-goose chases.

I will offer you a series of thoughts, or statements, and as you hear them, pay attention to the way you feel. Does the statement hook you up to the faucet or disconnect you from it?

"Okay."

Look at that poor old woman. She can barely walk.

"Well, that feels bad, Solomon."

I just don't know what will happen to Aunt Zoie. She can barely get up the stairs now. What will she do when she gets worse?

"That unhooks me, Solomon. That's easy."

I wonder where her rotten children are. Why don't they come here and take care of her?

"I've wondered that, Solomon. And you're right. That unhooks me, too."

Aunt Zoie is a strong old woman. I think she likes her independence.

"Hmm. That thought feels better."

Even if someone did try to take care of her, she probably wouldn't like that.

"Yes. That thought feels better, too. And that's probably true, Solomon. She gets mad at me when I try to do things for her." Sara remembered how annoyed Aunt Zoie became when Sara impatiently tried to finish her sentences.

This wonderful old lady has lived a long, full life. I have no way of knowing that she is unhappy.

"That feels good."

She may very well be living exactly as she wants to live.

"That feels good, too."

I'll bet she has lots of great stories to tell about things she has seen. I'll stop and visit with her every now and again and find out.

"That feels very good, Solomon. I think Aunt Zoie would like that."

You see, Sara, you can look at the same subject, in this case the subject of Aunt Zoie, and find many different conditions to focus upon. And you can tell by the way you feel whether you're choosing a condition that is helpful or one that is not.

Sara felt so much better. "I think I'm beginning to understand this, Solomon."

Yes, Sara, I believe you are. Now that you're consciously wanting to understand this, it's my expectation that you will have many opportunities to figure it out. Have fun with this, Sara.

ఌఌఌ

CHAPTER 21

Things just seemed to be getting better and better. Every day seemed to have many more good things within it than bad things.

I'm so glad that I have found Solomon. Or that Solomon has found me, Sara pondered, as she walked home from a day of school that had not included one negative incident. *Life really is getting better and better for me.*

Sara stopped at her leaning perch on the Main Street bridge, and hanging way out over the swift-moving river, she smiled broadly. Her heart was truly singing, and all was very well in Sara's world on this day.

Hearing loud, boyish screeching, Sara looked up to see Jason and Billy running about as fast as she had ever seen them run. They were moving so fast, as they ran past her, that she decided they must not have even noticed that she was perched there. And she watched them holding on to their hats and running at top speed past Hoyt's store. Something about the way they were running made Sara laugh a little. They really did look sort of silly, running so fast that they had to hold their hats on. *Those two are always trying to break the sound barrier,* Sara smiled, but she noticed that they weren't bothering her nearly as much as they used to. They hadn't changed much, or really at all, but they weren't getting under Sara's skin anymore. Not like before.

Sara waved at Mr. Matson, who, as usual, had his head under the hood of someone's car, and then picked up her pace as she headed toward Solomon's thicket. "What a beautiful day!" Sara spoke right out loud, looking upward into a beautiful blue-skied afternoon and breathing in the fresh spring air. She usually found her spirits rising once the last snow was melted and the spring grasses and flowers began to grow. Winter was long here, but it wasn't the passing of winter that cheered Sara so, but the passing of school. Three months of freedom, looming in the immediate future, was always reason for Sara to be glad. But somehow Sara knew that this happy heart wasn't about school nearing another year's end. This was about Sara's discovery of her valve. She had learned to keep it open—anyway.

It feels so good to be free, Sara thought. *It feels so good to feel good. It feels so good not to be afraid of anything.*

"EEEEKKKKKK!" Sara shrieked, as she found herself jumping high in the air to avoid walking right into the biggest snake she had ever seen, stretched out to its full length, which seemed endless, across the roadway. Coming down well on the other side of it, Sara found herself running at a dead run, one full country block, not slowing in

the least, until she was certain she had left that snake far behind.

"Well, maybe I'm not as fearless as I thought I was," Sara laughed to herself. And then she began to laugh even harder as she realized what had caused Jason's and Billy's burst of speed and lack of desire to stop and pester her. Sara was still laughing and panting as she walked into Solomon's thicket.

Solomon was waiting, expectantly and patiently, for Sara. *Well, Sara, are you filled with some newfound enthusiasm today?*

"Solomon, strange things are happening to me these days. Just when I think I really understand something, something else happens to make me realize I don't understand it at all. Just when I decide that I'm truly brave and afraid of nothing, something pops up that scares me to death. Things are very weird, Solomon."

You don't seem to be scared to death, Sara.

"Well, I exaggerated a bit, Solomon, because, as you can see, I am not dead . . ."

What I meant was, you don't appear to be frightened. You seem to be laughing more than anything.

"Well, I am laughing now, Solomon, but I wasn't when that great big snake was lying in my path, just waiting to bite me. I had just been pointing out to myself how brave and fearless I am now, and then in the next moment I felt instant fear and began running for my life."

Oh, I see, Solomon replied. *Sara, don't be too hard on yourself. It's perfectly normal to have a strong feeling response when you're faced with a condition that's not pleasing in some way.* ***It's not your initial response to something that sets the tone of your vibration—or of your point of attraction—it's what you do with it later that has a lasting effect.***

"What do you mean?"

Why do you think the snake frightened you so, Sara?

"Because it's a snake, Solomon! Snakes are scary! Snakes

bite you and make you sick. They can even kill you. Some of them wrap around you and break your ribs and smother you so you can't breathe," Sara reported proudly, remembering the details from the scary nature film she had seen at school.

Sara stopped to catch her breath and tried to settle down a little bit. Her eyes were flashing and her heart was pounding.

Sara, do you think that these words that you're offering here are making you feel better or worse?

Sara had to stop and think for a moment because she wasn't even thinking about how her words were affecting her. She was just excited to explain how she felt about snakes.

You see, Sara, that's what I meant when I said that it's what you do next that is most important. As you're talking on and on about this snake and other snakes and all the bad things that snakes might do, you're holding yourself in that vibration—and it's becoming more and more likely that you will attract other uncomfortable experiences with snakes.

"But Solomon, what should I do? I mean, that big old snake was just lying there. And then I saw it. I almost stepped right on it. And then, there's no telling what it would have done to me . . ."

There you go again, Sara. you're still imagining—and holding as your image of thought—something that you do not want.

Sara was quiet. She knew what Solomon meant, but she

didn't know what to do about it. The fact of the snake was sooooo big and soooooo close and soooooo scary that she couldn't find another way to approach the subject. "Okay, Solomon, tell me what you would do if you were a little girl who almost stepped on a big snake."

Well, first of all, Sara, you have to remember that your goal is, first and foremost, to find a better feeling place. If you have any other goal, you will get very much off track. If you try to figure out where all of the snakes are, you will feel worse. If you decide to be so alert that you never see another snake up close, you will feel overwhelmed. If you try to learn to identify all snakes in order to label them good and bad, you will feel the impossible task of sorting all of that out. Sifting through the conditions will only make things worse. Your only goal is to try to approach this subject in a way that makes you feel better than you felt when you were jumping and running away from the snake.

"How would I do that, Solomon?"

You could say something to yourself like, "This big old snake is just lying there getting some sun. He is happy the winter is over, and the sun feels good to him, just like it feels good to me."

"I still don't feel better, though."

You could say something like, "This big old snake isn't the least bit interested in me. He didn't even look up as I ran by. He has many other things to do than bite little girls."

"Well, that does feel a little better. What else?"

"I sure am alert." Solomon continued. *"It's good that I saw the snake, or sensed it, and jumped over it so that I didn't bother it. The snake would do the same thing for me."*

"But would he, Solomon? How do you know that?"

Snakes live all around you, Sara. They are in the river. They are in the grasses where you walk. When you pass by, they get out of your way. They understand that there is enough room for everyone. They understand the perfect balance of your physical planet. They have their valves open, Sara.

"Snakes have valves?!"

They certainly do. All of the beasts of your planet have valves. And their valves are wide open most of the time.

"Hmm," Sara pondered. She was feeling much better, now.

You see, Sara, how much better you feel? Nothing has changed. The snake is still lying right where you last saw him. The condition hasn't changed. But the way you feel certainly has.

Sara knew that Solomon was right.

Sara, from now on when you think of snakes, you will feel positive emotion. Your valve will be open, their valve will be open. And you will continue to live in harmony.

Sara's eyes shined bright with her new understanding. "Okay, Solomon. I'd better go. I'll see you tomorrow."

Solomon smiled as Sara skipped down the path. Then Sara stopped and yelled back over her shoulder, "Solomon, do you think I'll ever be afraid of snakes again?"

Well, maybe, Sara. But if you're ever frightened, you know what to do about it.

"Yeah," Sara grinned, "I do."

And eventually, Solomon added, *your fear will be completely gone. Not only about snakes, but about everything.*

As Sara walked home from the thicket, she looked off into the new spring grasses alongside the road, and she

wondered how many snakes were hiding there. At first, she shivered a little at the frightening thought that snakes were hiding in the bushes along all of her private trails, but then she thought about how nice they had all been to stay hidden and out of her way. How nice they had all been not to jump out and scare her like Jason and Billy so often did.

Sara smiled as she walked up her driveway and into her yard. She felt triumphant and strong. It felt good to leave fears behind. It felt really, really good.

~~~
~~~

CHAPTER 22

"Sara! Sara! Wow, Sara! Guess what? We found Solomon!"

Oh, no, that can't be! Sara thought, as she stood, frozen, on the street as Jason and Billy came speeding toward her on their bicycles.

"What do you mean, you found Solomon? Found him, where?"

"We found him over on Thacker's Trail, Sara. And guess what else?" Jason announced proudly. "We shot him!"

Sara felt so weak that she thought she would fall down. Her knees nearly buckled right out from under her.

"He was just sitting there on this post, Sara. So we flushed him up into the sky, and then Billy shot him with his BB gun. It was awesome, Sara! But he's not nearly as big as we thought he would be. He's mostly feathers."

Sara could not believe her ears. The impact of what she was hearing was so intense, so very important, and Jason was driveling on about Solomon not being as big as he thought he would be? Sara felt as if her head would explode. Her book bag dropped to the ground, and Sara began to run as fast as she had ever run in her life, to Solomon's thicket.

"Solomon! Solomon! Where are you, Solomon?!" Sara cried out, frantically.

Here, Sara, I'm here. Don't be alarmed.

And there, lying in a rumpled clump, was Solomon.

"Oh, Solomon!" Sara cried, as she fell down on her knees in the snow. "Look at you! Look what they've done to you!"

Solomon was truly a mess. His always neat feathers were rumpled and seemed to be going in every direction, and the pure white snow all around Solomon was red with blood.

"Solomon, Solomon, what should I do?"

Sara, this is no big thing, really.

"But Solomon, you're bleeding. Look at all of this blood. Are you going to be all right?"

Of course, Sara. Everything is always all right.

"Oh, Solomon, please don't give me more of that 'all-is-well' junk. I can see, very well, with my own eyes, that all is not well!"

Sara, come here to me, Solomon said.

Sara crawled right down next to Solomon and put her hand on his back and stroked the feathers under his chin.

This was the first time that Sara had actually touched Solomon, and he felt so soft and so vulnerable. Tears rolled down Sara's cheeks.

Sara, don't get this rumpled pile of bones and feathers mixed up with who Solomon really is. This body is only a focal point—or a point of perspective—for something much more to see through.

Your body is the same, Sara. It isn't really who you are. It's just the perspective that you use, for now, to allow who you really are to play and grow and rejoice.

"But, Solomon, I love you. Whatever will I do without you?"

Sara, wherever do you get this stuff? Solomon isn't going anywhere. Solomon is forever!

"But, Solomon, you're dying!" Sara blurted, hurting more than she could ever remember hurting.

Sara, listen to me. I am not dying, because there is no such thing as death. True, I won't be using this body for now, but it was getting old and a bit stiff anyway. I've had a real crick in my neck ever since the day I tried to turn my head all the way around to please the Thackers' grandchildren.

Sara laughed through her tears. Solomon could nearly always make her laugh, even in the worst of times.

Sara, our friendship is forever. And that means that anytime you would like a chat with Solomon, all you have to do is identify what you want to talk about, focus upon it, bring yourself to a place of feeling very good—and I'll be right here with you.

"But will I see you, Solomon? Will I be able to see you and touch you?"

Well, probably not, Sara. Not for a while, anyway, but Sara, that's not what our relationship is about, anyway.

We are mental friends, you and I.

And with those last words, Solomon's crumpled body relaxed into the snow, and his big eyes fluttered shut.

"No!!!!!" Sara's voice echoed across the pasture. "Solomon, don't leave me!"

But Solomon was quiet.

Sara stood up, looking down at Solomon's body. He looked so small, lying there in the snow, his feathers moving softly in the wind. Sara took off her coat and laid it on the snow next to Solomon. She lifted him gently onto her coat and wrapped it around him. And then, not noticing that it was really quite cold, Sara carried Solomon down Thacker's trail.

Sara, our friendship is forever. And that means that anytime you would like a chat with Solomon, all you have to do is identify what you want to talk about and focus upon it, bring yourself to a place of feeling very good, and I'll be right here with you, Solomon said again—but Sara couldn't hear.

~~~
~~~

CHAPTER 23

Sara didn't know what to do or where to begin to explain to her parents who Solomon was, or the important friend he had come to be to her. Her mind was spinning, and she was filled with regret that she hadn't told her family more about her owl friend, because now she had no way to explain the tragedy that had befallen her. She had turned entirely to Solomon for guidance and comfort, and had all but severed those kinds of ties with her own family, and now she found herself faced with the loss of Solomon. She felt truly alone, with no place to turn.

She didn't know what to do with Solomon. The ground was still so frozen and hard that she knew she couldn't manage to dig a grave for him. The thought of tossing him into the coal furnace, in the furnace room, as she had seen her father do with dead birds or mice, was just too awful to even think about.

Sara was still sitting on the front steps of her house, holding Solomon in her arms, with tears flooding down her face, when her father's car skidded to a quick stop on the graveled driveway. He came rushing out of the car carrying Sara's wet book bag and crumpled pile of books. Sara had forgotten all about her things, left on the side of the road.

"Sara, Mr. Matson called me at work. He found your bag and books on the side of the road. We thought something had happened to you! Are you all right?"

Sara wiped at her wet face, embarrassed to have her father see her like this. She wanted to somehow hide Solomon, to continue to keep him a secret, and at the same time, she wanted, so much, to somehow find some comfort in telling her father everything.

"Sara, what has happened? What's wrong, sweetheart?"

"Oh, Daddy," Sara blurted. "Jason and Billy have killed Solomon."

"Solomon?" her father questioned, as Sara opened her coat to let him see her dead friend.

"Oh, Sara, I'm so sorry." He had no idea why this dead owl was so significant to her, but it was clear that Sara was experiencing real trauma. He had never seen his daughter like this before. He wanted to take her in his arms and kiss her hurt away, but he knew that whatever had happened here was much too big for that. "Sara, give Solomon to me. I'll dig a grave for him behind the chicken coop. Go inside and get warm."

Only then did Sara realize how very cold she was. She reluctantly released her precious bundle and put Solomon in her father's arms. Sara felt weak, so sad, and so very tired. She stayed seated on the steps as she watched her father gingerly carry her beautiful Solomon out of view. She smiled limply through her tears as she noticed how seriously and delicately her father was carrying this feathered bundle, somehow seeming to understand how valuable it was.

Sara flopped onto her bed, still fully clothed. She kicked her shoes off onto the floor and sobbed into her pillow and then fell asleep.

~~~
~~~

CHAPTER 24

Sara found herself standing in some strange thicket, surrounded by beautiful spring flowers, with bright-colored birds and butterflies flying all around her.

Well, Sara, it seems that you have much to talk about today, Solomon quipped.

"Solomon!" Sara shouted with glee. "Solomon, you're not dead, you're not dead! Oh, Solomon, I'm so glad to see you!"

Sara, why are you so surprised? I told you there is no death.

Now, Sara, what is it you want to talk about? Solomon offered calmly, as if nothing out of the ordinary had happened.

"Solomon, I know that you said that there is no such thing as death, but you looked dead. You felt limp and heavy, your eyes were shut, and you weren't breathing."

Well, Sara, you just became used to seeing Solomon in a certain way. But now you have an opportunity—because your wanting is so much greater than ever before—to see Solomon in a broader way. A more universal way.

"What do you mean?"

Well, most people see things only through their physical eyes, but you now have the opportunity to see things through broader eyes—more through the eyes of the true Sara that lives within the physical Sara.

"You mean there is another Sara living inside of me, like you're the Solomon who lives inside of my Solomon?"

Yes, Sara, that's it. And that Inner Sara lives on forever and ever. That Inner Sara will never die, just as this Inner Solomon that you see here will never die.

"Well, that sounds very good to me, Solomon. Will I see you back on Thacker's trail tomorrow?"

No, Sara, I will not be there.

Sara frowned.

But think about it, Sara! Whenever you wish to chat with Solomon, you may. No matter where you are. You don't have to walk to the thicket anymore. You have only to think of Solomon—and remember what it feels like to visit with Solomon—and I'll be right here to visit with you.

"Well, that sounds okay, Solomon. But I've loved our visits in the thicket. Are you sure you wouldn't just as soon go back there, like before?"

Sara, you'll come to like our new way of interacting even more than you have loved our fun in the thicket. There is no limitation in our new way of interacting. You'll see. We'll have great fun.

"Okay, Solomon. I believe you."

Good night, Sara.

"Solomon!" Sara cried out, not wanting Solomon to leave her so soon.

Yes, Sara?

"Thank you for not being dead."

Good night, Sara. All is well.

PART II

The Happily Forever Afterlife of Sara and Solomon

Chapter 25

"Solomon, aren't you mad at Jason and Billy for shooting you?"

Why, Sara? Why would I want to be mad at them?

"Well, Solomon, they shot you!" Sara replied in amazement. How could Solomon not understand her question, and how could he not be mad at them for doing something so awful?

No, Sara. Whenever I think of Jason and Billy, I just appreciate them for bringing you to me.

"But Solomon, don't you think that shooting you is more significant than that?"

Sara, the only thing that is significant is that I feel good. And I cannot feel anger toward them and feel good at the same time. ***Keeping my valve open is most significant, Sara—so I always choose thoughts that feel good.***

"Solomon, wait a minute. Are you saying that no matter how bad someone is, and no matter what sorts of awful things they do, you do not think about those things? That nobody ever does anything bad enough to make you mad at them?"

Sara, they all mean well.

"Oh, Solomon, come on. They shot you! How bad does it have to get before you understand how bad that is?"

Sara, let me ask you some questions. Do you think that if I got really, really mad at Jason and Billy for shooting me that they would stop shooting things?

Sara was quiet. She didn't think that Solomon's anger would make any difference. She had been angry at the boys countless times for shooting things, and it had never even slowed them down.

"No, Solomon. I guess not."

Can you think of any purpose that my anger would serve?

Sara thought about that, too.

If I became angry at them, it might make you feel more justified in your anger, Sara, but then I would only be joining your chain-of-pain, and no good could come from that.

"But, Solomon," Sara protested, "it just seems like—"

Sara, Solomon interrupted, *we could talk all day and all night about which actions are right and which actions are wrong. You could spend the rest of your lifetime trying to sort out which behaviors are appropriate and which are not, and under which conditions they are appropriate and under which conditions they are not appropriate. But what I have learned is that any time, even if it's one minute, that is spent trying to justify why I feel bad, is wasted life. And I have also learned that the faster I can get to a place of feeling good, the better my life is—and the more I have to offer to others.*

So, through lots of living and lots of experiencing, I have come to know that I can choose thoughts that close my valve or I can choose thoughts that open my valve—but in every case, it's ***my*** *choice. And so I gave up blaming the Jasons and Billys long ago, because it didn't help me—and it didn't help them.*

Sara was quiet. She was going to have to think about this one. She had already decided that she would *never* forgive Jason for this terrible deed, and here Solomon was, unwilling to join her, even one little bit, in her blame.

Remember, Sara, if you let the conditions that surround you control the way you feel, you will always be trapped. But when you're able to control the way you feel—because you control the thoughts you offer—then you're truly liberated.

Sara remembered hearing something like that from Solomon before, but then, nothing this big was challenging them. Somehow this seemed too big to forgive.

Sara, in this big world where so many people have different ideas of what is right and wrong, you will often be faced with witnessing behavior that you may feel is inappropriate. Are you going to demand that all of those people change their ways just to please you? Would you want to do that, even if you could?

The idea of everyone behaving in a way that would please her did appeal to Sara in some ways, but she truly didn't think that that was a likely thing. "Well, no, I guess not."

Then what is the alternative? Will you hide yourself away, shielding yourself from witnessing their diverse behavior, making yourself a prisoner in this beautiful world?

Well, that option was really not to her liking, but Sara recognized remnants of that behavior in her not-so-distant past, as she often, mentally, had withdrawn from others, crawling into her own mind, keeping all or most of them outside. *Those weren't happy times,* Sara remembered.

Sara, you will experience such joy when you're able to keep your valve open, anyway. When you're able to acknowledge that many people are choosing different things; they believe differently; they want differently; they act differently, and when you understand that all of that adds to a more perfect whole, and that none of that threatens you—because the only thing that affects you is what you're doing with your own valve—then you move about freely and joyously.

"But Solomon, Jason and Billy did more than threaten you. They shot you. They killed you!"

Sara, you're still not over that, are you? Can you not see that I am not dead? Sara, I am very much alive. Did you think that I would want to live in that tired, old body of an owl forever?

Sara knew that Solomon was teasing her, because he was neither tired-seeming or old.

It is with great joy that I released that physical body, knowing that whenever I want to, I can pour my Energy into another, younger, stronger, faster one.

"You mean, you wanted them to shoot you?"

It's co-creation, Sara. That's why I let them see me. So that they could co-create this very important experience. Not only for me, but for you, too, Sara.

Sara had been so overwhelmed with all that had happened since Solomon's shooting that she had not had time to wonder how it was that Jason and Billy were able to see Solomon.

The important thing to understand, Sara, is, first: All is truly well, no matter how it may seem to you from your physical perspective. And second, whenever your valve is open, only good things can come to you.

Sara, try to appreciate Jason and Billy as I do. You will feel much better.

When pigs fly, Sara thought. And then she laughed at her own negative response. "I'll think about it, for you. But this is so different from anything I've ever thought about before. I've always been taught that when someone does something wrong, they should be punished."

The problem with that, Sara, is that all of you have a difficult time deciding who gets to decide what is wrong. Most of you believe that **you** *are right; therefore, they must be wrong. Physical beings have been killing each other for years, arguing about that one. And with wars and killings that have been taking place on your planet for thousands of years, you still have come to no agreement.*

You would all be much better off if you would just pay attention to your own valves. Life would be much better, right away.

"Do you think people will be able to learn about their valves? Do you think everyone will learn that?" Sara felt overwhelmed with the enormity of this endeavor.

That doesn't matter, Sara. For the only thing that matters to you, is that ***you*** *learn it.*

Well, that didn't seem so big. "Okay, Solomon, I'll work on this some more."

Good night, Sara. I have enjoyed our visit immensely.

"Me, too, Solomon. Good night."

~~~
~~~

Chapter 26

Jason and Billy sped by Sara on their bicycles, calling out something obnoxious and inaudible. Sara smiled as they passed her by, and then she felt a little bit of surprise as she realized that they would disappoint her if they failed to be as bad as they could be, and that, in some strange way, the three of them were co-creators in this game they were always playing together. The game of "I'm your rotten little brother, and this is my obnoxious, rotten little friend, and our task is to make your life miserable in every way we can, and your job is to respond to us in misery."

This is weird, Sara thought. *I'm not supposed to enjoy them. Whatever could be happening here?*

As Sara continued to walk toward home, out of habit she almost turned the corner to go to Solomon's thicket, forgetting, temporarily, that that was no longer their meeting place. That thought reminded Sara of Solomon's shooting, and that thought reminded Sara of Solomon's response to being shot by these two rotten little boys. And then a very strong awareness came over Sara.

Jason and Billy shot Solomon, and Solomon still loves them. Solomon is able to keep his valve open even under those conditions, so maybe I'm learning to keep my valve open, too. Maybe my life is finally important enough to me that I am not bothered by what others are doing or saying.

Goose bumps bumped up all over Sara's body. She felt light and tingly all over—and she knew that she'd figured something out that was very significant.

That's good, Sara. I agree with you wholeheartedly. Sara heard Solomon's voice.

"Hi, Solomon. Where are you?" Sara asked, still longing for a visual Solomon to gaze upon as she chatted.

I'm here, Sara, Solomon replied, sliding past the question quickly, and getting on to more important business. *Sara, you have just stated the most important secret of life. You are coming to understand what unconditional love really is.*

"Unconditional love?"

Yes, Sara, you're coming to understand that you're a lover. you're a physical extension of pure, positive Nonphysical Energy, or love. And as you're able to allow that pure love Energy to flow, no matter what, in spite of the conditions that surround you—then you have achieved unconditional love. You are then, and only then, truly the extension of who you really are and who you have come here to be. You are then, and only then, truly fulfilling your purpose for being. Sara, this is very good.

Sara felt elated. She wasn't completely understanding the magnitude of what Solomon was saying, but she could tell, from the enthusiasm with which he was saying it, that it must be really important, and she was certain that Solomon was very pleased with her.

Well, Sara, I know this sounds a bit strange to you in the beginning. It's a whole new orientation for most people, but until you understand this, you will never truly be happy. Not for long, anyway.

Sit here and just listen for a little while, and I'll explain to you how it all works.

Sara found a dry, sunny spot and plopped herself down to listen to Solomon. She loved listening to the sound of his voice.

There is a Stream of pure, positive Energy that flows to you at all times. Some may call it Life Force. It's called many different things, but it's the Stream of Energy that created your planet to begin with. And it's the Stream of Energy that continues to sustain your beautiful planet. This Stream of Energy keeps your planet spinning in its orbit in perfect proximity to other planets. This Stream maintains the perfect balance of your microbiology. This Stream

maintains the perfect balance of water on your planet. This is the Stream that keeps your heart pumping, even when you're asleep. This is a wonderful, powerful Stream of Well-being, Sara, and this Stream flows to each of you every minute of your day and night.

"Wow," Sara sighed, as she tried to understand this wonderful, powerful Stream.

As a person living on your planet, Sara, in any moment, you can allow or resist this wonderful Stream. You can let it flow to you and through you, or you can disallow the Stream.

"Why would anyone not want this Stream?"

Oh, everyone would want it, Sara, if they understood it. And no one ever resists it on purpose. They just have habits that they have learned from each other that cause resistance to this Stream of Well-being.

"Like what, Solomon?"

Well, Sara, the main thing that causes people to be resistant to the Stream of Well-being is their looking at the evidence that has been created by others who have been resistant to the Stream of Well-being.

Sara looked puzzled. She wasn't really getting this yet.

You see, Sara, whenever you give your attention to anything, just by observing it you begin to vibrate as it is—while you're observing it. So if you're looking at sickness, for example, for the time you're looking at or talking about or thinking about sickness, you're not allowing the Stream of Well-being. You have to look at Well-being to allow Well-being.

Sara began to brighten. "Ah! This is like that birds-of-a-feather stuff we talked about before, isn't it?"

That's right, Sara. It's about the Law of Attraction. If you want to attract wellness, you must vibrate with wellness. But if you give your attention to someone's sickness, you cannot allow wellness at the same time.

Sara began to pucker as she thought about what Solomon was saying. "But Solomon, I thought I was supposed to help people who are sick. And how can I help them if I don't look at them?"

It's okay to look at them, Sara, but don't see them as sick. See them as getting better. Better yet, see them as well, or remember them when they were well. That way, you don't use them as your reason to stop the Stream from flowing to you.

It's not easy for people to hear this, Sara, because they're so conditioned to observing everything around them. If they only knew that when they look at things that make them feel negative emo-

tion, that that feeling is their signal that they have just disallowed the Stream of Well-being, I do not think so many people would be so willing to look at so many things that make them feel bad.

Sara, just for a moment here, don't try to understand what most others are doing. Just listen to this. There is one constant, steady Stream of Well-being, and it's flowing to you at all times. When you feel good, you're allowing the Stream, and when you feel bad, you're not allowing the Stream. Now, when you understand that, what is it that you want most to do?

"Well, I want to feel good as much as I can."

Good. Now, let's say you're watching television and you see something that makes you feel bad.

"Yeah, like when somebody gets shot or killed or hurt in an accident?"

Yes, like that. When you see that, Sara, and you feel bad, do you understand what is happening?

Sara smiled brightly. "Yes, Solomon, I am resisting the Stream."

You've got it, Sara! Whenever you're feeling bad, you're resisting the Stream. Whenever you're saying no, you're pushing against, and therefore resisting, the Stream.

Sara, when someone says no to cancer, they are actually disallowing the Stream of Well-being. When someone says no to murderers, they are actually disallowing the Stream of Well-being. When someone says no to poverty, they are actually resisting the Stream of Well-being—because when you're giving your attention to what you don't want, you're vibrating with it, which means you're resistant to what you do want. So, the key is to identify what you don't want, briefly, but then to turn to what you ***do*** *want and say* ***yes.***

"That's it?! That's all we have to do? Just say ***yes*** instead of ***no!***" Sara couldn't believe how simple this all sounded. She felt elated. "Solomon, that is so easy! I can do that! I think everybody could do that!"

Solomon enjoyed Sara's enthusiasm about this new knowledge. *Yes, Sara, you can do that. And that is what you have come forth to teach to others. Practice it for a few days. Pay attention to yourself and others around you, and notice how practiced most of you are at saying* ***no*** *to things much more often than you say* ***yes*** *to things. As you observe, for a while, you will come to understand the sorts of things that people do to resist the Well-being that is natural. Have fun with this, Sara.*

~~~
~~~

CHAPTER 27

All the next day, Sara's thoughts kept drifting back to what she and Solomon had last talked about. Sara was truly excited about coming to understand something that Solomon seemed to think was so very important, but the more time that elapsed since her conversation with Solomon, the more she wasn't sure at all that she had understood what Solomon was trying to teach her. Sara did remember, though, that Solomon encouraged her to observe others, to see how much more often they said no than yes, so Sara decided to pay close attention to that.

"Sara, I don't want you to be late tonight," her mother warned. "We're having company for dinner, and I'll need you. We don't want our company to visit us in a messy house now, do we?"

"Okay," Sara sighed, reluctantly. Company was not her favorite thing. Not even close to her favorite thing.

"Now, Sara, I mean it. Don't be late!"

Sara stopped in the doorway, happily surprised to have found some evidence, so early in the morning, that supported what Solomon had said. She moved slowly, sort of staring off into the distance as she reviewed what she could remember of Solomon's words, unknowingly letting cold air fill the living room as she stood in the open doorway.

"Sara! Don't stand there letting cold air in! For heaven's sake, Sara, get going. You're going to be late for school."

Wow! Sara mused. It was amazing. Her mother had just, in the last two minutes, offered five clear statements of what she didn't want, and Sara couldn't remember even one statement about what her mother did want. And the amazing thing was, her mother didn't even notice what she was doing.

Sara's father was just finishing pushing snow from the front sidewalk when Sara skipped down the front steps. "Be careful, Sara. The walkway is slippery. You don't want to fall."

Sara grinned from ear to ear. *Wow,* she thought. *This is amazing!*

"Sara, did you hear me? I said, watch out or you will fall down."

Sara didn't actually hear her father saying no to anything, but his words certainly were pointed at what he didn't want.

Sara's mind was spinning. She wanted to speak what she

did want. "I'm okay, Daddy," she said. "I never fall down." *Whoops,* Sara thought. *That wasn't exactly saying yes.*

Wanting to be the best example that she could be for her father, Sara stopped and turned directly to her father and said, "Thank you, Daddy, for keeping the walkway clear for us. It makes it easy for me to not fall down."

Sara laughed right out loud as she heard herself, even when she was deliberately trying to say yes, still talking about not falling down. *Boy,* Sara thought, *this is not going to be easy.* And then again she laughed and then said right out loud, in amazement at herself, "Not going to be easy? Good grief, Solomon, I see what you mean."

Sara was only about 200 yards from her driveway when she heard the front door of her house slam shut, and she turned to see Jason running at top speed, holding his book bag in one hand and holding his hat on with the other hand, fast approaching Sara. Sara could see, from the fast approach Jason was making, and from the gleam she recognized in his eyes, that he was about to brush Sara from behind, as he had done dozens of times before, just enough to set her off balance and to make her mad. And, in anticipation, Sara shouted, "Jason don't you dare . . . Jason, *no*, darn you, Jason, don't doooooo that!" Sara shouted with all her might.

Good grief, Sara thought. *I'm doing it again. "No" just keeps coming out of me, even when I don't want it to.* ***Don't*** *want it to? There I go again.* Sara felt almost frantic. She couldn't seem to control her own words.

Jason brushed past Sara and kept on running, and as he was now over a block ahead of her, Sara began to relax into her own quiet walk to school and to reflect on the amazing events that she had observed over the past ten minutes.

Sara had decided to make a list of the "nos" that she had heard so that she could sort it out later with Solomon. Taking her little notebook from her book bag, Sara wrote:

DON'T BE LATE.

DON'T WANT A MESSY HOUSE.

DON'T LET COLD AIR IN.

DON'T BE LATE FOR SCHOOL.

DON'T WANT TO FALL DOWN.

NOT GOING TO BE EASY.

JASON, DON'T YOU DARE.

Sara heard Mr. Jorgensen shouting at two boys in her classroom, "Don't run in the hallway!" Sara wrote it in her book. She was leaning up against her locker when another teacher from another classroom walked past her and said, "Hurry up; you're going to be late." Sara wrote that down, too.

Sara sat in her seat, trying to settle into another long day in school, when she saw the most amazing sign posted at the front of the classroom. The sign had been there all of this school year, but Sara hadn't noticed it before. Not like she was noticing it now. She could barely believe her eyes. She took out her notebook and began writing what she was reading:

NO TALKING IN CLASS.

NO GUM CHEWING.

NO FOOD OR DRINK IN THE CLASSROOM.

NO TOYS ALLOWED.

NO SNOW BOOTS IN THE CLASSROOM.

NO STARING OUT THE WINDOW.

NO LATE WORK PERMITTED.

NO PETS ALLOWED IN THE CLASSROOM.

TARDINESS NOT PERMITTED.

Sara sat stunned. *Solomon is right. Most of us do resist our Well-being.*

Sara was eager to hear and observe as much as she could that day. During lunchtime, she sat by herself away from the other kids, listening to the conversation two teachers were having at the table behind her. She couldn't see them, but she could clearly hear them.

"Oh, I don't know," one teacher said. "What do you think?"

"Well, I wouldn't do it if I were you," the other teacher replied. "You never know. You could end up much worse off than you are now."

Wow, Sara thought. She had no idea what they were talking about, but one thing was absolutely clear: The advice was *no* to whatever it was.

Sara added to her list:

I DON'T KNOW.

I WOULDN'T DO IT IF I WERE YOU.

Sara wasn't halfway through this school day, and she already had two pages of nos to discuss with Solomon.

Sara's afternoon proved as fruitful as her morning as she

added to her list:

DON'T THROW THAT!

STOP THAT!

I SAID NO!

CAN YOU NOT HEAR ME?!

AM I NOT MAKING MYSELF CLEAR?

NO PUSHING!

I'M NOT GOING TO TELL YOU AGAIN!

By the end of the day, Sara was absolutely exhausted. It seemed to Sara that the whole world was resisting its Well-being.

"Boy, Solomon, are you ever right. Most everybody is saying no instead of yes. Even me, Solomon. I know what I'm supposed to do, and I can't even do it."

"I CAN'T DO IT." Sara wrote on her list.

What a day this had been.

That's quite a list you have there, Sara. You've had a busy day.

"Oh, Solomon, you don't know the half of it. This is only some of what I heard today. People are mostly saying "no," Solomon. And they don't even know it! And me, too, Solomon. This is hard."

Well, Sara, it really isn't so hard once you know what to look for and once you realize what your goal is. Sara, read something to me from your list, and I'll show you what I mean.

"DON'T BE LATE."

Be on time.

"DON'T WANT COMPANY TO VISIT A MESSY HOUSE."

We want our home to be comfortable for our guests.

"DON'T LET COLD AIR IN."

Let's keep our house nice and warm.

"DON'T BE LATE FOR SCHOOL."

Being on time really feels best.

"DON'T WANT TO FALL DOWN."

Stay focused and coordinated.

"NOT GOING TO BE EASY."

I'll figure this out.

"DON'T RUN IN THE HALLWAY."

Be considerate of others.

"NO TALKING IN CLASS."

Let's discuss and learn together.

"NO STARING OUT THE WINDOW."

Your full attention will truly be of tremendous benefit to you.

"NO LATE WORK PERMITTED."

Let's stay current and work together.

"NO PETS ALLOWED IN THE CLASSROOM."

Your pets are much happier at home.

"Gosh, Solomon, you're really good at this."

Sara, you'll be good at it, too. It just takes practice. And, Sara, the words that you use are not so very important. It's the feeling of ***pushing against*** *that is detrimental. When your mother said, "Don't leave the door open," she was certainly* ***pushing against*** *what she didn't want. But even if she had said, "Close the door!" she was still more aware of what she didn't want, and therefore, still, her vibration would have been one of pushing against.*

I'd like you to get the idea of relaxing toward what you do want, rather than pushing against what you do not want.

Certainly, your words are an indicator of your direction, but the way you feel is even a more clear indicator of your allowing or resisting.

Just have fun with this, Sara. ***When you push against saying no, you're still pushing against. The idea is just to talk more and more about what you do want.*** *And as you do that, things will just get better and better. You'll see.*

~~~
~~~

CHAPTER 28

Sara walked home on this the last day of school for this year with a strange combination of feelings. Usually, this was the happiest time of her year, having a full summer of near solitude ahead of her, not being forced to mix with a room full of different, and often uncomfortable, classmates. But on this year, the last day felt different to Sara. She had changed so very much in this very short year.

Sara walked briskly, breathing in the wonderful spring air, looking ahead, and then walking backwards for a while. She was eager to see everything and everyone around her. The sky was more beautiful than she had ever remembered seeing it. Bluer. Deeper in color. And the fluffy white clouds, in such stark contrast, were absolutely stunning. Sara could hear the sweet, clear songs of birds that were far enough away that she couldn't see them, but their perfect songs were reaching her ears anyway. The feel of the wonderful air upon her skin was truly delicious. Sara was walking in a state of true ecstasy.

So you see, Sara, Well-being truly does abound.

"Solomon, it's you!"

It's everywhere. Solomon's clear words continued in Sara's head.

"It is everywhere, Solomon. I can see it and feel it!"

In fact, it's everywhere that it is not disallowed. A constant, steady Stream of Well-being flows to you at all times, and, in any moment, you are allowing it or resisting it. And you're the only one who can allow or resist this constant, steady Stream of Well-being.

In all of the time that we have been visiting, the most important thing that I have wanted you to learn is the process of reducing, or eliminating, the patterns of resistance that you have learned from other physical people. Because, if it wasn't for the resistance that you have picked up along this physical trail, the Well-being that is natural to you, certainly the Well-being that you deserve would flow naturally to you. To all of you.

Sara thought back on all of the wonderful conversations she'd had with Solomon. How wonderful their interactions had been! And Sara realized that in every case, with every single conversation they had experienced together, Solomon had been helping Sara to lower resistance.

She thought back on the techniques, or games, that Solomon had offered day after day, and now, from her clearer perspective, she realized that, all along, Solomon had been teaching her processes to lower resistance.

Little by little, Sara had learned to leave her resistance behind.

You, too, are a teacher, Sara.

Sara's eyes widened, and she felt breathless, as her favorite teacher of all time announced that she, like Solomon, was a teacher. Sara felt that warm feeling of appreciation sweep through her and around her.

And what you have come to teach, Sara, is that all really is well. Through the clarity of your example, many others will come to understand that there truly is nothing to push against. And that, in fact, the pushing against is the reason for not allowing the Well-being.

Sara could feel a special intensity about Solomon's words. His words were thrilling Sara. She didn't know what to say.

She walked up her graveled driveway and into her front yard feeling so wonderful she wanted to leap into the air. Then she bounded up the front steps and into the house. "Hi, I'm home!" Sara called, to anyone who might be inside.

~~~
~~~

Chapter 29

Sara went to bed early, eager to get back to her conversation with Solomon. She closed her eyes and breathed deeply as she tried to find that wonderful place where she and Solomon had left off. "All really is well," Sara said aloud, with a calm, clear voice of absolute knowing. And then she opened her eyes in amazement.

Solomon, who Sara hadn't seen in weeks, was now hovering just above her bed. But his wings weren't moving at all. It was as if he was suspended in air, effortlessly hanging just above Sara's head. "Solomon!" Sara shouted in glee. "I am sooooo glad to see you!"

Solomon smiled and nodded.

"Solomon, you're so beautiful!"

Solomon's feathers were snow white and glowed as if each were a tiny spotlight. He seemed so much bigger and so much brighter, but it was Sara's Solomon all right. She could tell that by looking deep into his eyes.

Come fly with me, Sara! There is so much I want you to see!

And even before Sara could speak her agreement, she felt that incredible whoosh that she had felt before when she had flown with Solomon, and they were off, but this time they were high above her little town. In fact, they were so high above her town that she didn't recognize anything she saw.

Sara's senses were dramatically heightened. Everything she saw was amazingly beautiful. Colors were deeper and more wonderful than she had ever seen. The smell in the air was intoxicating; never had Sara beheld such wonderful fragrances. Sara could hear beautiful sounds of birds singing and water flowing and wind whistling. The sounds of wind chimes and happy children's voices were wafting around her. The feel of the air on her skin was soothing and comforting and exciting. Everything looked and smelled and sounded and felt delicious.

"Solomon," she said, "it's all so beautiful!"

Sara, I want you to know the utter Well-being of your planet.

Sara couldn't imagine what Solomon had in store for her, but she was ready and willing to go anywhere he wanted her to go. "I'm ready!" Sara exclaimed.

And in a flash, Sara and Solomon flew far from planet Earth, out, out, out beyond the moon, beyond the planets, and even beyond the stars. In an instant, they had traveled, what must have been light years, to where Sara could see her beautiful planet turning and glistening far off in the distance, moving in a sort of perfect rhythm with the moon and other planets and stars and the sun.

As Sara looked at the planet Earth, a feeling of total Well-being filled her little body. She watched with a sense of pride as the earth turned steadily and certainly on its axis, as if it were dancing with other partners, all of whom knew exactly their part in the magnificent dance.

Sara gasped in amazement.

Look at it, Sara. And know that all is well.

Sara smiled and felt that warm wind of appreciation envelop her.

The same Energy that created your planet, to begin with, still flows to your planet to sustain it. A never-ending flow of pure, positive Energy is flowing to all of you at all times.

Sara looked at her planet with complete knowing that this was true.

Let's take a closer look now, Solomon said.

Now Sara couldn't see any of the other planets, but planet Earth was glowing radiantly within her full view.

She could clearly see the dramatic definition between the land and the seas. The shorelines looked as if they had been emphasized with a giant marking pen, and the water shimmered as if there were millions of lights beneath it, lighting the seas just for her viewing from her heavenly perspective.

Do you know, Sara, that the water that has been nurturing your planet for millions of years is the same water that nurtures your planet today? That is Well-being, Sara, of immense proportion.

Think about it, Sara. Nothing new is being trucked or flown into your planet. The immeasurable resources that exist continue to be rediscovered by generation after generation. The potential for glorious life remains constant. And physical beings discover, to varying degrees, that perfection.

Let's look closer.

Solomon and Sara swooped down over the sea. Sara could smell the wonderful sea air, and she knew that all was well. They soared faster than the wind over the great Grand Canyon—a large, long, jagged crack in the Earth's crust.

"What is that?!" Sara gasped in amazement.

That is evidence of your Earth's constant ability to keep its balance. Your Earth is continually seeking balance. That is evidence of that.

Now, flying around at about the same distance from the Earth that the airliners flew, Sara enjoyed the incredible landscape below. So much green, so much beauty, so much Well-being.

"What is that?" Sara questioned, pointing at the little cone protruding from the surface of the Earth and puffing big clouds of gray and black smoke.

That's a volcano, Solomon replied. *Let's get a closer look.* And before Sara could protest, off they went, diving down closer to the Earth, flying right through the smoke and dust.

"Wow!" Sara shouted. She was amazed at her feeling of absolute Well-being even though the smoke was so dense she couldn't see one thing in front of her. They flew up and out of the smoke, and Sara looked down to see this amazing volcano spitting and spewing.

That is more evidence of Well-being, Sara. It's another sign that your Earth is managing to keep its perfect balance.

And then they flew, up, up, up, again, and off to another amazing sight. It was a fire. A very big fire. Sara could see what looked like miles of red and yellow flames, hidden at times by big clouds of smoke. The wind was blowing hard, and the smoke would sometimes clear, leaving quite a good view of the flames, and then get so dense that Sara couldn't see the flames at all for a while. Every now and again, Sara would get a glimpse of an animal running very fast away from the fire, and she felt sad that the fire was destroying the beautiful forest and the homes of so many animals.

"Oh, Solomon, that is just awful," Sara whispered, responding to the conditions she was witnessing.

That is only more evidence of Well-being, Sara. It's more evidence of your Earth seeking its balance. If we could stay here long enough, you would see how the fire will add much-needed nutrition to the soil. You would see new seeds germinating and thriving, and in time, you would see the amazing value of this fire, which is part of the overall balance of your planet.

"I'm just sad for the animals who are losing their homes, I guess."

Don't be sad for them, Sara. They are guided to new homes. They feel no lack. They are extensions of pure, positive Energy.

"But some of them will die, Solomon," Sara protested.

Solomon just smiled, and then Sara smiled, too.

It's hard to get over that "death thing," isn't it? All is very well here, Sara. Let's explore some more.

Sara loved the feeling of Well-being that was enveloping her. She had always thought of the sea as treacherous, with sharks and shipwrecks. The television reports that she had seen of volcanoes spewing forth had always frightened her. The news was always full of forest fires and disasters, and Sara realized now that she had been pushing hard against all of them.

This new point of view felt ever so much better. These things that Sara had always assumed were terrible, or tragedies, now took on an entirely new meaning when seen through the fresh eyes that Solomon had given her.

Sara and Solomon flew all night long, stopping to observe the amazing Well-being of Sara's planet. They saw a baby calf being born and baby chickens kicking their way out of eggs. They saw thousands of people driving in cars, and only a few of them bumping into each other. They saw thousands of birds moving to warmer climates and some farm animals growing longer hair for the winter. They saw gardens being harvested and other gardens being planted. They saw new lakes forming and new deserts forming. They saw people and animals being born, and they saw people and animals dying—and in every bit of every bit of all of it, Sara knew that all really was well.

"Solomon, how ever will I ever explain this to anybody? How will I ever make them understand?"

Sara, that's not your work. It's enough, sweet girl, that you understand.

Sara sighed a big sigh of relief, and then she felt her mother shaking her, "Sara, get up! We have lots to do." Sara opened her eyes to find her mother bending over her, and as she emerged into wakefulness, she pulled the covers over her head, wanting to hide from this day.

All truly is well, Sara. Sara heard Solomon's words. *Remember our journey.*

Sara pulled the blankets down from her head and smiled the most beautiful smile at her mother.

"Thanks, Mom!" Sara said. "I'll be fast as the wind. It will be all right. You'll see. I'll be ready in a flash."

Her mother stood stunned as she watched Sara bound from her bed, moving with deftness and clarity, and, most obviously, in joy.

Sara threw open her curtains, raised up her window, and stretched out her arms with a big smile on her face. "What a beautiful day!" she exclaimed, with such enthusiasm that her mother stood bewildered, scratching her head.

"Sara, are you all right, sweetheart?"

"I am perfect!" Sara said clearly. "All truly is well!"

"Well, if you say so, honey," Sara's mother said tentatively.

"And I do," Sara said, rushing in to the bathroom and smiling from ear to ear. "I do say so!"

THE END

About the Authors

Esther and **Jerry Hicks,** the *New York Times* best-selling authors of *Ask and It Is Given, The Amazing Power of Deliberate Intent,* and *The Law of Attraction,* produce the leading-edge Abraham-Hicks teachings on the art of allowing our natural Well-Being to come forth. While presenting open workshops in up to 60 cities per year, the Hickses have now published more than 700 Abraham-Hicks books, cassettes, CDs, videos, and DVDs.

Their internationally acclaimed Website is: **www.abraham-hicks.com.**

Other Hay House Titles for Young Readers

The Adventures of Lulu,
by Louise L. Hay and Dan Olmos

Incredible You!
by Dr. Wayne W. Dyer, with Kristina Tracy

The Journey Home, Children's Edition,
by Theresa Corley

Unstoppable Me!
by Dr. Wayne W. Dyer, with Kristina Tracy

All of the above are available at your local bookstore, or may be ordered by contacting Hay House (see next page).

We hope you enjoyed this Hay House book.
If you'd like to receive a free catalog featuring additional
Hay House books and products, or if you'd like information about the
Hay Foundation, please contact:

Hay House, Inc.
P.O. Box 5100
Carlsbad, CA 92018-5100

(760) 431-7695 or (800) 654-5126
(760) 431-6948 (fax) or (800) 650-5115 (fax)
www.hayhouse.com® • www.hayfoundation.org

Published and distributed in Australia by: Hay House Australia Pty. Ltd., 18/36 Ralph St., Alexandria NSW 2015 • *Phone:* 612-9669-4299 • *Fax:* 612-9669-4144 • www.hayhouse.com.au

Published and distributed in the United Kingdom by: Hay House UK, Ltd., 292B Kensal Rd., London W10 5BE • *Phone:* 44-20-8962-1230 • *Fax:* 44-20-8962-1239 • www.hayhouse.co.uk

Published and distributed in the Republic of South Africa by: Hay House SA (Pty), Ltd., P.O. Box 990, Witkoppen 2068 • *Phone/Fax:* 27-11-706-6612 • orders@psdprom.co.za

Published in India by: Hay House Publishers India, Muskaan Complex, Plot No. 3, B-2, Vasant Kunj, New Delhi 110 070 • *Phone:* 91-11-4176-1620 • *Fax:* 91-11-4176-1630 • www.hayhouseindia.co.in

Distributed in Canada by:
Raincoast, 9050 Shaughnessy St., Vancouver, B.C. V6P 6E5 • *Phone:* (604) 323-7100 • *Fax:* (604) 323-2600 • www.raincoast.com